Seven Deadly Sins of Organizational Culture

This book is about the primary symptoms present in a dysfunctional culture that could have devastating outcomes for any organization. The book outlines each of the seven sins in each chapter.

Each of the first seven chapters (Chapters 1–7) starts with a famous quote related to each of the sins and then immediately recounts stories ripped from the headlines describing well-known corporate failures but with a personal touch from former employees who experienced those stories from inside the company (The sources for these stories are all cited in their Bibliographies).

The seven sins of organizational culture are linked with seven different corporate scandals that serve as a "lesson learned" as well as seven stories of organizations that have been successful with each respective organizational attribute as follows:

1. Flawed Mission and Misaligned Values uses WorldCom as the lesson learned and Patagonia as the success case.
2. Flawed Incentives uses Wells Fargo as the lesson learned and Bridgeport Financial as the success case.
3. Lack of Accountability uses HSBC as the lesson learned and McDonald's as the success case.
4. Ineffective Talent Management uses Enron as the lesson learned and Southwest Airlines as the success case.
5. Lack of Transparency uses Theranos as the lesson learned and Zappos as the success case.
6. Ineffective Risk Management uses the 2008 mortgage industry collapse as the lesson learned and Michael Burry as the success case.
7. Ineffective Leadership summarizes all of the foregoing sins as failures of leadership.

In each chapter and for each organizational sin, the author offers seven attributes of a healthy culture to counter the cultural dysfunction. The seven healthy attributes for each of the seven sins are all original content.

In Chapter 8, the author offers an approach for assessing an organization's culture by providing seven ways to measure the different drivers of organizational culture. The ideas for how to measure corporate culture is original content, with some references to existing frameworks (all cited in the Bibliography).

Finally, in Chapter 9, the author offers a step-by-step outline for transforming the culture. The chapter starts with a story about how Korean Air suffered multiple crashes due to their corporate culture but were able to successfully transform their culture (The source for the Korean Air story is cited in the Bibliograhy).

There are seven appendices, most of which are by the author except for the maturity of risk management, which references an OECD (government entity) risk management maturity framework.

Security, Audit and Leadership Series
Series Editor: Dan Swanson, Dan Swanson and Associates, Ltd., Winnipeg, Manitoba, Canada.

The ***Security, Audit and Leadership Series*** publishes leading-edge books on critical subjects facing security and audit executives as well as business leaders. Key topics addressed include Leadership, Cybersecurity, Security Leadership, Privacy, Strategic Risk Management, Auditing IT, Audit Management and Leadership

Artificial Intelligence Perspective for Smart Cities
Vahap Tecim and Sezer Bozkus Kahyaoglu

Teaching Cybersecurity: A Handbook for Teaching the Cybersecurity Body of Knowledge in a Conventional Classroom
Daniel Shoemaker, Ken Sigler and Tamara Shoemaker

Cognitive Risk
James Bone and Jessie H Lee

Privacy in Practice: Establish and Operationalize a Holistic Data Privacy Program
Alan Tangsss

Leading the Digital Workforce
Jeff Brown

Controlling Privacy and The Use of Data Assets V II: What is the New World Currency – Data or Trust?
Ulf Mattsson

Security Risk Management - The Driving Force for Operational Resilience: The Firefighting Paradox
Jim Seaman and Michael Gioia

Cybersecurity Operations and Fusion Centers: A Comprehensive Guide to SOC and TIC Strategy
Kevin McLaughlin

Seven Deadly Sins of Organizational Culture: Lessons from Some of The Most Infamous Corporate Failures
L.T. San

The Change Agent: Transforming an Underperforming Internal Audit Department
Hernan Murdock

https://www.routledge.com/Security-Audit-and-Leadership-Series/book-series/CRCINTAUDITA

Seven Deadly Sins of Organizational Culture

Lessons From Some of The Most Infamous Corporate Failures

L.T. San

CRC Press
Taylor & Francis Group
Boca Raton London New York

CRC Press is an imprint of the
Taylor & Francis Group, an **informa** business

Cover Image Credit: Shutterstock

First edition published 2024
by CRC Press
2385 NW Executive Center Drive, Suite 320, Boca Raton, FL 33431

and by CRC Press
4 Park Square, Milton Park, Abingdon, Oxon, OX14 4RN

CRC Press is an imprint of Taylor & Francis Group, LLC

ISBN: 978-1-032-26546-9 (hbk)
ISBN: 978-1-032-26547-6 (pbk)
ISBN: 978-1-003-28878-7 (ebk)

DOI: 10.1201/9781003288787

Typeset in Caslon
by SPi Technologies India Pvt Ltd (Straive)

Contents

Preface

I didn't know it at the time, but something happened in 2001 that would prove to have a profound impact on my career in so many ways. That singular event, which triggered a series of related events to occur, was the demise of Enron. The collapse of this energy company, which once generated $100 billion in revenue at its peak, also brought down another company, Arthur Andersen (Pearlstein, 2001). As Enron's external auditors, Arthur Andersen had issued unqualified or "clean" audit opinions for the years 1997 through 2000; however, the company had to revise its financial statements for those same years to account for $586 million of previously undisclosed losses ("Timeline: A Chronology of Enron Corp", 2006). Enron ultimately filed for bankruptcy. In response to Enron, and several other accounting scandals which unfolded, the Sarbanes–Oxley (SOX) Act in 2000 was enacted to reform public company financial reporting practices, including the related internal financial controls as well as the financial reporting audit procedures performed by external auditing firms (Carlson, 2010).

So, how did these events affect me? The SOX Act brought with it a wave of transformational change to the audit profession – both the accounting firms that conduct external audits of publicly traded companies and the internal audit functions of public companies. My entire 30-year career thus far has been spent virtually all within the audit profession – initially for one of the "big four" accounting firms and then for the respective internal audit functions of five different companies. My first job out of college as a newly minted graduate was with KPMG, a competitor of Arthur Andersen. The year I graduated, KPMG was originally named Peat Marwick and they were one of the "big eight" accounting firms in 1991. That number has now dwindled to four firms (hence, the "big four") due to multiple mergers and the fall of Arthur Andersen. Having worked as an auditor for ten years before SOX and another 20 years after SOX became law, I was able to experience first-hand how it changed the entire landscape in both the audit profession and for public companies in general. To give you an idea of the sheer scale of the impact of this regulation, a frequently cited study estimates that the average cost per company in the first year of implementation of SOX was $1.6 to $4.4 million (Bialik, 2005). These are 2003 dollars. Apparently, the assertion that "Greed is good" from the movie *Wall Street* is also true for the audit and consulting firms, an industry that benefited significantly from burdensome government regulations.

Since the fall of Enron and enactment of SOX, there continues to be countless headlines featuring infamous new scandals on the world stage of corruption, including AIG, Lehman Brothers, Wells Fargo, and Theranos. This is not to say that having effective financial controls is a futile endeavor. Having effective internal controls is not just common sense but also one of the pillars of basic corporate governance. However, it has become increasingly clear that the passing of more laws has done little to prevent the next Enron. Regulation cannot change human behavior.

If, somehow, we could influence or change not just one individual's behavior but a group of people's behaviors, indeed, even all the people in a particular organization, it could be exceptionally valuable to any company. How do we change the behavior of a group of people to facilitate a desired outcome? What are the drivers of an organization's culture and how do we measure these attributes to determine if they are predictive of a healthy or unhealthy culture? If we could focus efforts from within the organization rather than passing more regulations imposed by government entities external to the organization, perhaps we can avoid another corporate failure as well as minimize the cost and burden of ever-increasing regulatory compliance. If we are to change behaviors, we must understand what drives behaviors.

Bibliography

Carl Bialik, "How Much Is It Really Costing To Comply With Sarbanes-Oxley?", *Wall Street Journal*, June 16, 2005. https://www.wsj.com/articles/SB111885041027560378

Rosemary Carlson, "The Enron Scandal That Prompted the Sarbanes-Oxley Act," *The Balance*, November 16, 2010, https://www.thebalancesmb.com/sarbanes-oxley-act-and-the-enron-scandal-393497#:~:text=The%20act%20was%20passed%20in,and%20corporate%20boards%20of%20directors.

Steven Pearlstein, "At Enron, the Fall Came Quickly," *Washington Post*, December 2, 2001, https://www.washingtonpost.com/archive/politics/2001/12/02/at-enron-the-fall-came-quickly/d699dbdd-2694-409a-8493-5f355ae9f148/

"Timeline: A Chronology of Enron Corp," *New York Times*, January 18, 2006, https://www.nytimes.com/2006/01/18/business/worldbusiness/timeline-a-chronology-of-enron-corp.html

About the Author

Linh San Truong (L.T. San), MBA, CPA, CIA, CISA, has extensive experience encompassing 30 years of corporate governance, risk, and control frameworks in public accounting as well as leadership roles in multiple industries including financial services, oil/gas, and healthcare. Ms. Truong is a Certified Public Accountant (CPA), Certified Internal Auditor (CIA), and a Certified Information Systems Auditor (CISA).

Ms. Truong's experience includes positions with KPMG and Credit Suisse Group as well as consulting for a Fortune 20 multinational conglomerate. As the Chief Audit Executive (CAE) for three of her former employers, she established the inaugural enterprise risk management initiatives and launched their respective internal audit functions from ground zero. Her audit career spans much of North America, Europe, as well as North and West Africa. She currently serves as the CAE and is a member of the executive leadership team at North Texas Tollway Authority.

Ms. Truong is a professional speaker who has been invited to speak on the topic of organizational culture at multiple Institute of Internal Auditors events and conferences, including the General Audit Management Conference in 2019 and the International Conference in 2020.

The topics of her many speaking engagements also include Enterprise Risk Management, Agile Auditing, and Fraud/Anti-corruption.

Ms. Truong has authored several published articles including *Assessing Corporate Culture* for the Business Transformation and Operational Excellence Insights Report and *Agile Auditing: More Value, Less Resources for the EDP Audit, Control, and Security Newsletter.*

Introduction

It's hard to argue that human behavior, at least at work, is driven in large part by the culture of the organization. If organizational culture drives behaviors, then it is logical to conclude that a healthy culture would result in positive behaviors. Culture is an intangible concept. It's often described as something ubiquitous. It is the "DNA" or "soul" of the company. It's not surprising that few people have attempted to craft an approach for evaluating it, much less measuring it. So, how can you assess and measure the health or "wellness" of an organization's culture? After all, you can't manage what you don't measure. As with any form of assessment, you typically need to know the current state, know the desired state, and find the gaps between the current and desired state. Once you identify the gaps, you can start to develop and implement action plans for closing those gaps to achieve a desired or target state.

I deliberately chose the term "wellness" because I like to use the analogy of going to the doctor to receive regular wellness checks as preventative maintenance. An ounce of prevention is worth a pound of cure, as they say. At a wellness check, doctors check your heart rate, blood pressure, cholesterol level, body mass index, etc. because all these things evaluated collectively are a measure of good or poor health. If the results from this health assessment are outside the "normal range", then the abnormal results could be a leading indicator of more serious health issues such as an impending heart attack, stroke, diabetes diagnosis, etc. If a person diligently goes for their annual health checkup, their doctor could identify negative trends in test results, while signs of more serious health issues are still in the early stages and preventable. The doctor could then prescribe the appropriate medication, diet, and exercise to "correct course" before a health crisis becomes inevitable.

Most public companies are currently undergoing annual checkups in the form of audits from their external auditors; unfortunately, these checkups are focused primarily on the financial statements and the related financial controls. Continuing with the analogy, that would be similar to the doctor only looking at our blood pressure or only looking at our weight to determine if we are healthy individuals. It is not a comprehensive evaluation of the whole being or entity. Although financial controls are very important, it is but only one measure of a company's health.

How do we then holistically measure the wellness of an organization's culture? In this book, I am proposing that there are, at the very least, seven key drivers of organizational culture from which there could be seven "deadly sins" of a toxic organizational culture:

1. Flawed Mission and Misaligned Values
2. Flawed Incentives
3. Lack of Accountability
4. Ineffective Talent Management
5. Lack of Transparency
6. Ineffective Risk Management
7. Ineffective Leadership

To be clear, there is no new quantitative data collected for this book. The primary reason for this is simple: there is no need for new data or information. There is an overabundance of real-world examples of organizations that suffered negative consequences and, in some cases, met their tragic ends, as a result of a broken culture. Every lesson that can be learned on the topic of toxic cultures has already happened many times over again. The seven sins have been committed by well-known companies and already been documented in official court documents, first-hand accounts written from former employees, countless articles with interviews conducted by journalists, and facts already researched, checked, and published by various reputable news media and publishers.

One of the best ways to learn lessons is through telling stories. The real stories recounted in this book have already been told by others – they are merely cited and referenced here. The information is there and freely accessible to anyone to connect the dots. What is new are the lessons learned or drawn from an observer of history and the offerings of a remedy or cure for these organizational sins.

Although the stories are mostly corporate fraud and corruption-related stories ripped from headlines, this is not a book about fraud. At its heart, it is a book about organizational culture. Bad things happen when organizations have a dysfunctional culture. Rampant fraud and corruption are just some of those bad outcomes. The hope is that the world can learn from all historical mistakes. Because if we don't learn from history, we are doomed to repeat it.

1
Flawed Mission and Misaligned Values

"Life is only meaningful when we are striving for a goal"/"Virtue is only known by its acts"

– Aristotle

The date was June 17 in the summer of 2002 (Cooper, 2008). After months of investigating what would eventually amount to nearly $4 billion of expenses that were being capitalized, Cynthia Cooper and Glyn Smith were walking toward David Myer's office, WorldCom's Controller, to ask about these unusual accounting entries (Romero & Berenson, 2002). Cynthia was WorldCom's Chief Audit Executive and Glyn was her second in command. When asked about these entries, David began talking about the company's cost structure being so high and that, if it doesn't change, "we might as well shut the company down".

"Do you have support for these entries?", Cynthia asked David.

"No, I could go back and construct support, but I'm not going to do that," David said calmly.

"How were the amounts for the entries derived?", Glyn asked.

"They were booked based on what the margins should be", he answered matter-of-factly.

"Are there any accounting standards supporting the entries?", Cynthia asked David.

"No, there are no specific accounting standards supporting the line costs." David said. He then added, "We probably shouldn't have capitalized the line costs. But once it was done the first time, it was hard to stop."

DOI: 10.1201/9781003288787-1

These words were extracted and paraphrased from Cynthia Cooper's book *Extraordinary Circumstances*. Cooper wrote in her book a first-hand account of how WorldCom committed fraud by overstating assets by a staggering $11 billion. At the time, it was the single largest corporate accounting fraud case in US history (George, 2021). Several executives and the CEO were indicted on charges of securities fraud, conspiracy, and filing false documents with regulators. The company ultimately filed for bankruptcy and what remained of the company was purchased by Verizon in 2006.

Lessons Learned: WorldCom

When a company, especially one as large as WorldCom, ceases to exist, one could ponder what impact the company made? Will the world feel the absence of this entity? Or will their demise merely benefit their competitors who will absorb their customers? What was the company's mission? WorldCom's mission statement was simple: "Our objective is to be the most profitable, single-source provider of communications services to customers around the world" (Cooper, 2021). At face value, WorldCom's stated mission was about turning a profit. Even the statement's reference to their customers seemed to be merely a means to an end. It isn't very clear, at least not in this one line of their mission statement, how they would improve the lives of their customers with their services. There was also no reference to how they would serve other stakeholders, whether that be their shareholders, employees, suppliers, or the communities and environment in which they operate. Maximizing their profit was their sole mission or, at least, that was what their mission statement seemed to suggest. Even with such a narrow mission statement, they failed at being a profitable entity. Their mission statement was arguably flawed from the beginning.

A company's mission statement should provide clarity behind an entity's "why". In one or two sentences, it should explain the purpose of the organization's existence. Everything you do as a company should work toward your mission statement. So, what makes a good mission statement? Here are a few examples of mission statements deemed by Forbes to be some of the most "inspiring" ones (Valentine, 2018):

- "Organize the world's information and make it universally accessible and useful." – Google
- "Build the best product, cause no unnecessary harm, use business to inspire and implement solutions to the environmental crisis." – Patagonia
- "Entertain, inform and inspire people around the globe through the power of unparalleled storytelling, reflecting the iconic brands, creative minds and innovative technologies that make ours the world's premier entertainment company." – Disney

If an organization has an inspiring mission, then their employees would be inspired to come to work for more than just a paycheck – they come to work because they are committed to the mission. This commitment is what fosters a culture that will endure. An organization's mission is its north star that guides their strategy and all the activities that execute that strategy. A flawed mission is the first deadly sin of organizational culture. Redemption comes in the form of the following attributes for a mission that is more conducive to a healthy culture:

- An organization's mission is universal or at least implicitly inclusive of all key stakeholders.
- An organization's mission states what it is they do that makes the world a better place.
- An organization's mission has goals that inspire other companies.
- An organization's mission should be formally documented.
- An organization's mission should be communicated to all employees and stakeholders.
- An organization's strategy should support its mission.
- An organization's strategy should be achievable within the boundaries of its values.

An Organization's Mission Is Universal or at Least Implicitly Inclusive of All Stakeholders

As the world awaits global guidance for environmental, social, and governance (ESG) related standards of reporting, the shift from an organization's focus on shareholders to all key stakeholders is well underway. After all, it is counterintuitive to believe that catering to any one specific stakeholder could sustain long-term success when other stakeholder interests are marginalized, deprioritized, or outright ignored. When there is a significant disparity in the flow of benefits to the privileged few versus the larger majority who are negatively impacted, there is a tipping point that ultimately disrupts the status quo. For example, Patagonia's mission not only explicitly includes the environment as a stakeholder but actually uses the term "crisis" in reference to it. The point is to be as universal and inclusive in the organization's mission as possible. In 2006, NASA removed mention of Earth from its mission statement, changing from "To understand and protect our home planet..." to simply "To pioneer the future in space exploration, scientific, discovery, and aeronautics research," thereby removing any limits in their endeavor to any one specific planet in the universe ("7 examples of strong & effective mission statements").

An Organization's Mission States What They Do That Makes the World a Better Place

For every company that gets their mission statement right, there are so many more that get it wrong. Many of the less-inspiring ones include the typical "be number one or top company" among their peers or "grow/dominate" the industry or, like WorldCom, make a lot of revenues/profits for their shareholders. None of these missions explain how this positively impacts the lives of people, particularly the customers or other key stakeholders. Some do get it right. For example, State Farm provides insurance. It could have easily formulated a mission statement that was straightforward since insurance is not intuitively an exciting or sexy subject matter. However, they managed to make it rather clear how they contribute to the world being a better place with a practical yet inspiring mission statement: "To help people manage the risks of everyday life, recover from the unexpected, and realize their dreams".

An Organization's Mission Includes Goals That Inspire Other Companies

Going above and beyond in one's mission means endeavoring to have both a direct and indirect impact. It should be fairly easy to communicate how an organization's services or products directly improve lives across the world. But is the organization's mission so aspirational that it aims to indirectly lead other organizations to achieve similar positive outcomes for the world? Such mission statements would be considered the best of the best. Warby Parker aspires to do just that with their mission statement: "To offer designer eyewear at a revolutionary price, while leading the way for socially conscious businesses" (Lagorio-Chafkin). These companies are setting the new higher standards for other companies to follow. In the words of Warby Parker's co-founder and co-CEO, Neil Blumenthal, "We wanted to be that example...We need more business leaders to be considering the impact of their products on all stakeholders...". The pinnacle of leadership is to not only be a leader within one's organization but also a leader for an entire industry or even for all businesses regardless of industry.

An Organization's Mission Should Be Formally Documented

Once a company has established their mission, it should be formalized. If something is important, you write it down. Important messages are put in writing so people don't have to rely on word of mouth among the masses where it can be misquoted, misconstrued, or misunderstood. Mission statements should be documented and institutionalized. You cannot hold people accountable for anything that's not formally documented.

An Organization's Mission Should Be Communicated to All Employees and Stakeholders

Once formalized, an organization's mission should be clearly communicated, both internally and externally, to all key stakeholders. For employees, even when things are written down, one cannot assume everyone will interpret the words in the same way or as the message was intended. Even prospective employees want to know what a company stands for before they make their decision to join the company. This is especially true for younger generations. They will eventually comprise most of the workforce and they are the ones who will inherit the planet. Understandably, they would like to know if the organization has a mission that is responsible and inclusive of all stakeholders including the planet. Even external stakeholders such as prospective investors are now more interested in sustainable investing. These investors are now incorporating measures for analyzing a company's approach to addressing environmental, social, and governance risks. Customers are also becoming more socially aware and are the court of public opinion whose judgment drives their purchasing decisions.

An Organization's Strategy Should Support Its Mission

The mission statement is the north star for the company's strategic objectives. The strategy drives the actionable initiatives that achieve the mission. The strategy may change over time but is always in alignment with the mission. The strategy then drives the goals and objectives for departments as well as for individual employees. Everyone should be rowing in the same direction guided by the organization's north star – the mission.

An Organization's Strategy Should Be Achievable within the Boundaries of Its Values

Although having the right mission is critical, almost as equally important is the manner in which the organization achieves that mission. Even a noble mission will be hollow if the organization encourages their employees to break laws to accomplish their mission. Companies can also comply with laws and still be unpopular with their stakeholders if they are not doing the "right" thing in terms of being a good corporate citizen. That is why it is important to have corporate values.

Once the mission statement has been developed, the organization now needs a set of principles that guide the manner in which they accomplish their mission. These principles are their core values. Across all organizations, large or small and regardless of industry, there are a set of core values I find to be most common to encourage healthy behaviors. As these values exhibited by employees become what the organization considers the "norm", the behaviors which are inconsistent with these values are quickly recognized as rogue outliers.

The most common characteristics in a set of good core values usually include the following:

- Inclusivity
- Collaboration
- Excellence
- Integrity
- Accountability
- Transparency
- Safety

Inclusivity A culture that encourages inclusivity is one that is tolerant. There is a high tolerance for accepting or at least entertaining different ideas. Such a culture provides a safe space (more on safety later) for different perspectives and, therefore, encourages innovative thinking. Different ideas typically come from people with a wide range of experiences which suggests a tolerance of diverse backgrounds, age groups, ethnicities, etc. The opposite of an inclusive culture is one that perhaps encourages group thinking and discourages contrarian thoughts. A culture that does not foster inclusivity is one that could more likely cause individuals to feel they do not belong or do not feel that their input is valued or empowered to even offer their input.

Collaboration Collaboration is critical to success. People are the most important resource to any organization. They are the ones who bring the ideas, build the tools and technology, and run all operations. Machines can only do so much and even machines are, after all, designed and built by people. However, anyone would be hard-pressed to identify any line of work or discipline that does not require teamwork. This means that a company can hire smart and hardworking individuals, but if they cannot effectively work together, the tasks, projects, and goals are probably not going to be achieved. This requires collaboration among employees. Without a collaborative culture, companies are more likely to produce "cliques" and "kingdoms" in individual departments with subcultures that deviate from the overall desired corporate culture. Silos within organizations have never been cited by anyone as playing a part in healthy cultures.

Excellence A culture of excellence does not necessarily mean that the organization executes perfectly all the time, but rather is one that always strives for continuous improvement. This implies that the culture is comfortable with self-reflection and has the humility to identify their flaws as well as the fortitude to resolve them. This would also suggest that the company is tolerant of employees who speak up and provides a safe place for constructive criticism against the status quo and the leaders who own the current state without fear of retaliation. Organizations can benefit greatly from providing an environment that genuinely welcomes the opportunity to continuously improve.

Integrity Integrity is about respect, not just for rules but for all things that the organization impacts. This includes respect for the mission that drives the company, the core values that guide the company, the employees that power the company and all the external stakeholders, including its customers, vendors/suppliers, the community, and even the environment in which it operates. It is a responsibility to do the right thing in all that the company touches. It is a constant balancing act that understands doing good for one group may have negative consequences for another group, but nevertheless, continuously seeks the path which results in the "most" good or the least harm for all involved.

Accountability A culture of accountability (more about accountability in a separate chapter) is simply one where leaders hold employees and each other accountable for their actions or inaction. Every organization has policies and rules, but it is what organizations do when employees break those rules that set them apart. If rules are ignored for high performers or are not consistently enforced, then there is a lack of accountability. If employees see that there are no consequences for breaking the rules, then they no longer respect the rules or the leaders who establish those rules.

Transparency There is no accountability without transparency (more about transparency in a separate chapter). Transparency is the discipline and willingness to share information within the company and to external stakeholders. Transparency involves sharing all the information that is necessary to make informed decisions and hold the organization accountable to what it has committed to do and how it is performing against the stated mission and goals. Included in the information it discloses should be data related to how well the company is doing in its efforts to do the "most good". This means more than just information about the company's financial health, but also the environmental and social impact as well as how it governs itself, or ESG matters.

Safety Safety exists on many levels. Employees work best in environments in which they feel safe: physically, financially, and psychologically. First and foremost, organizations need to provide a safe work environment, especially in high-risk industries such as construction, extractive, or manufacturing industries. There should be safety-related policies and procedures as well as training and equipment to keep employees physically safe. Financial safety means that companies provide compensation that is not only aligned with industry standards or meets regulatory minimums but actually provides a "living" wage. Employees working full-time but also needing to supplement their income with other jobs to live may be perfectly legal but may not be a positive reflection on the values of that organization. Psychological safety suggests that the work environment is respectful and not hostile. Companies can benefit from providing a psychologically safe environment by encouraging employees to speak up without the fear of retaliation as well as encouraging new and innovative ideas without the fear of ridicule.

Success Case: Patagonia

Can having a noble mission be profitable? Patagonia is proof positive that having a purpose beyond profits can indeed be profitable. Patagonia has prioritized people and the planet since its founding in 1973. The company's mission statement includes the words "we're in business to save our home planet" ("Patagonia proves purpose can be profitable", 2021). The company has proven that it pays to have a responsible purpose as the retailer reached a record-breaking $10 million sales during their recent Black Friday sales. These results were five times greater than what the company had initially predicted. True to its stated mission, the company donated every penny to hundreds of environmental organizations around the world.

Patagonia's founder, Yvon Chouinard, is taking this purpose to an extreme (Gelles, 2022). He and his family have irrevocably transferred all the company's voting stock, equivalent to 2% of the overall shares, into a newly established entity known as the Patagonia Purpose Trust. The trust is intended to ensure that Patagonia makes good on its commitment to run a socially responsible business and give away its profits. The family then donated the other 98% of the company to a newly established nonprofit organization called the Holdfast Collective, which will now be the recipient of all the company's profits and intends to use the funds to combat climate change.

It is easy for any company to write an inspiring mission and advertise a list of noble core values. Companies can communicate them internally to all employees and publish them externally on their websites for the world to see. The difficulty lies in living out the mission and embedding the values into the day-to-day behaviors of each employee. How do organizations motivate, indeed incentivize, employees to do the right things? We explore ways to do this in the next chapter.

Bibliography

7 examples of strong & effective mission statements," https://thinkmonsters.com/speakinghuman/media/7-mission-statements/

Cynthia Cooper, *Extraordinary Circumstances*. New Jersey: John Wiley & Sons, 2008.

Cynthia Cooper, "Whistle Blowing: A Case by Cynthia Cooper," *Ivy Panda*, November 9, 2021, https://ivypanda.com/essays/whistle-blowing-a-case-by-cynthia-cooper/

David Gelles, "Billionaire No More: Patagonia Founder Gives Away the Company," *The New York Times*, September 21, 2022, https://www.nytimes.com/2022/09/14/climate/patagonia-climate-philanthropy-chouinard.html

Betsy George, "Fraudulent accounting and the downfall of WordCom," *USC Audit & Advisory Services*, August 11, 2021, https://www.sc.edu/about/offices_and_divisions/audit_and_advisory_services/about/news/2021/worldcom_scandal.php

Christine Lagorio-Chafkin, "Warby Parker had a mission. Its customers didn't care. Here's how the company changed its message," *Inc.*, https://www.inc.com/christine-lagorio/warby-parker-neil-blumenthal-founders-project.html

"Patagonia proves purpose can be profitable," *Business Chief*, December 2, 2021, https://businesschief.com/sustainability/meet-company-patagonia-proves-purpose-can-be-profitable

Simon Romero and Alex Berenson, "WorldCom says it hid expenses, inflating cash flow $3.8 billion," *New York Times*, June 26, 2002, https://www.nytimes.com/2002/06/26/business/worldcom-says-it-hid-expenses-inflating-cash-flow-3.8-billion.html

Gerry Valentine, "Want to make your company resilient? Start with an inspiring mission," *Forbes*, April 11, 2018, https://www.forbes.com/sites/forbescoachescouncil/2018/04/11/want-to-make-your-company-resilient-start-with-an-inspiring-mission/?sh=265db3062412

2
Flawed Incentives

> *"The superior man understands what is right, the inferior understands what will sell"*
>
> *–Confucius*

This was going to be her big break, she thought to herself (Arnold, 2016). She hadn't even finished college yet, but she was starting her first day as a personal banker at the Wells Fargo's branch located at the corporate headquarters. Her parents were so proud of her. She recalled being so excited that she overdressed, wore stiletto heels, and had on a pound of hairspray in her hair. What she thought would be her dream job quickly turned into a nightmare when she realized that employees were expected to sell at least eight products a day. During a sales push called "Jump into January", employees were expected to sell 20 products a day. When employees couldn't meet their sales goals, they were called into conference rooms for "coaching sessions", sternly reprimanded, issued formal warnings, and threatened with the real possibility of being fired which would be in their permanent record. She experienced these coaching sessions herself and became so distraught after one particularly harsh session that she threw up in the wastebasket under her desk. The former Wells Fargo employee did not want her name sourced in the news article. Other employees corroborated the stories which included witnessing employees leave coaching sessions in tears. The interviews with former employees conducted in 2016 consistently painted a picture of a "pressure-cooker" sales environment in which the bank pushed their employees to deceive customers in an effort to meet aggressive sales goals. John Stumpf, the former Wells Fargo CEO once said "There was no incentive to do bad things" in reference to the accounting scandal. Although this may be true, there were certainly many reasons why the structure of the incentive-based compensation and the sales environment resulted

DOI: 10.1201/9781003288787-2

in the unintended consequence of the employees' unethical activities. When all was said and done, the company generated approximately 3.5 million fake accounts (Sweet, 2017).

Lessons Learned: Wells Fargo

How a company incentivizes its employees can significantly impact their behavior. This one driver of behavior is, in my professional opinion, the strongest driver. Think about it. The authority to take away someone's source of income, their livelihood, is a powerful one. It's the power to impact someone's ability to pay their rent or mortgage, put food on the table for their families, keep their electricity and water running, or send their kids off to college for a better life. A job is tied to one's identity, self-respect, and dignity. It's all those things. And these decisions do not just impact them, but also their families. From the employer's perspective, it's just business. But from the employee's perspective, it's easy to see that this is very personal.

People will behave the way an organization pays them to behave. Therefore, companies should not incentivize bad behaviors. This seems to be an obvious statement, yet some companies have clearly made these exact mistakes at substantial financial and reputational costs to their organizations. Companies do not typically set out to motivate their employees to commit fraud. But incentive compensation can be a slippery slope that leads companies down a path of unintended consequences. Wells Fargo was merely trying to incentivize their employees to open more accounts with customers to increase the company's revenues. So, how did things go so wrong?

First and foremost, employee goals should be reasonably achievable. The goal for bank employees to sell eight accounts per customer was extremely aggressive considering the industry average was only 2.7 products per customer (Colvin, 2017). Apparently, the sales quota metric of eight accounts per customer at Wells Fargo was not based on any sort of peer benchmarking data but was chosen because the number "eight" rhymes with "great", making it a catchy slogan of "Eight is great" (Witman, 2018). Adding to the unrealistic sales goals was an intense pressure to achieve those targets which included daily and weekly status calls as well as threats of demotions and terminations if those quotas were not met.

If Wells Fargo was attempting to dangle a treat in front of their employees, it wasn't a very healthy one. Instead of a "carrot", it was more like candy. It certainly tasted sweet and was temporarily pleasing, but it was not nutritional in terms of long-term value and health for the organization. It achieved the goal of increasing the number of accounts per customer as well as increasing profits, to some extent, at least temporarily.

These millions of fraudulent accounts opened by the employees were mostly shell accounts. These fake accounts were not actively used since customers were not even aware these accounts were opened in their names on their behalf. The flawed incentive compensation structure merely added mostly empty accounts with minimal or no funding at all. Most of these accounts (approximately 75%) were later eventually closed once customers became aware of these unwanted accounts opened in their name (Witman, 2018). Not only did many of these accounts fail to bring additional funds to the bank, but there was an incremental administrative cost to the bank for opening and maintaining these accounts regardless of the level of activity or funding. In the end, Wells Fargo had to pay $3 billion in fines and penalties to regulatory authorities for opening these fraudulent accounts (Kelly, 2020). Even more costly was the damage to the company's reputation which is far more difficult to quantify and repair.

The sales targets set by the bank were not based on any actual increase in the value of their customer accounts, but rather based on a certain number of accounts. The incentive compensation structure was based on the quantity of customer accounts opened and not the quality of those accounts. Banks don't make money from the number of accounts. They make money from the amount of funds in those accounts. So, if increasing profitability was their goal, they may have been using the wrong metric to drive their employee incentive compensation.

By changing the incentive compensation metric from being based on quantity to one based on quality, Wells Fargo could have been more aligned with the company's values at the time. In addition, by focusing on the quality of sales, the organization would facilitate the corporate objective of increasing profitability rather than just sales. At a minimum, incentive programs based on volume should be risk-adjusted. There should be an offsetting metric to the volume-based incentive to discourage attempts to "game" the system in order to attain the target goals at all costs (i.e., resorting to fraud). In other words, the risks associated with achieving a certain goal should be identified. Those risks should then be mitigated by incorporating different goals to discourage employees from accepting more risk than is deemed acceptable. This would be the "stick". The Wells Fargo fraudulent accounts incident occurred a decade ago, so they may have already changed their incentive compensation for the better since then.

When I worked in the oil and gas industry, revenues were driven by only two factors: volume (of oil produced) multiplied by the market price (of a barrel of oil). Since we didn't have much control over the market price, the only way to generate more revenues was to produce more oil out of the ground (or buy up other oil companies that produced oil). There was a lot of pressure to produce as much oil in a day as operationally possible. However, it was a dangerous business. There was always the risk of a blowout if we were overzealous and moved too quickly by shortcutting any of the required safety procedures which were speedbumps on the highway leading to our production goals. Optimizing the balance of speed and safety was a constant challenge. The CEO made sure everyone's bonuses were based on both metrics. There was one bonus metric based on the volume of barrels that the company produced for the year. This was the "carrot". But there was also a safety metric to ensure that everyone complied with health and safety regulations. If the safety metrics weren't met, everyone's bonuses got docked. This was the "stick". The offsetting metrics attempted to ensure employees didn't ignore or skip safety rules in efforts to achieve the volume-based bonus metric. This way, employees understood very well that if they sacrificed safety to attain production goals, everyone's bonuses would be negatively impacted. Since no one wanted their bonuses to be reduced by a safety incident, everyone was very mindful and disciplined about following safety regulations.

Imagine if banks used incentive compensation metrics that were aligned with long-term value rather than just short-term volume or quantity of sales. Along those lines, there could have been a focus on more qualitative attributes for financial institutions to consider for their incentive compensation, including:

- The amount of actual dollars in funding in each customer account
- The actual interest earned per customer
- The number of credit cards or loans (offset by late payments or defaults)

Instead of focusing on just the *number* of accounts opened, they could have focused on the *quality* of the accounts opened. This type of transactional data was probably already being captured by their systems; however, these metrics did not appear to be selected as primary drivers of their incentive compensation campaign.

Healthy Attributes: Incentive Compensation

If incentivizing bad behavior is one of the deadly sins of organizational culture, then redemption comes in the form of the following attributes for incentive compensation that would be more conducive to a healthy culture:

- Incentive compensation should align with organizational values.
- Incentive compensation structures should establish target goals that are achievable.
- Incentive compensation structures should be risk-adjusted.
- Incentive compensation should focus on quality, not quantity, or at least not just quantity.
- The "carrots" and "sticks" should apply to everyone – no exceptions.
- Incentive compensation should avoid unintended consequences.
- Incentive compensation structures should be reevaluated and revised as needed.

Incentive Compensation Should Align with the Organizational Values

Every company needs to make money to survive. Revenue and profit goals are necessary for companies to continue to operate and grow. If organizations are not growing, then they are dying. Nonetheless, companies need to decide what values they are committed to upholding in their pursuit of those goals. Those values need to be incorporated into the company's incentive programs. For example, if being ethical is a core value, then opening accounts on behalf of customers without their permission would not be in line with this value. Pressuring employees to achieve unrealistic goals with the threat of termination would also not be in line with this value.

Incentive Compensation Structures Should Establish Target Goals That Are Achievable

Metrics for incentive compensation targets should be based on data-driven information. For example, companies should evaluate historical trends or industry benchmarking data to make informed decisions regarding realistic goals. Arbitrary metrics that are aggressive, unrealistic, and/or significantly exceed industry averages without plausible justification may encourage employees to take on risk that is unacceptable to the organization or even break laws.

Incentive Compensation Structures Should Be Risk-Adjusted

To mitigate the risks that may be associated with transaction- or volume-based incentives, there should be other metrics incorporated into the incentive compensation structure to discourage employees from accepting a level of risk that is not tolerable for the organization's risk appetite. For companies that are in the construction, manufacturing, mining, and energy industries or any other industry where safety is an inherently high risk, safety metrics are often used to ensure that employees are motivated to comply with safety standards. However, if there are more rules to follow, the pace of operations may inevitably be slowed. If the wheels on the machine turn slower, this may negatively impact growth or volume metrics which affects revenue. The answer is to have both types of metrics in place so that employees are encouraged to achieve growth but at a pace that is safe since they are incentivized to do both. Companies need to find the right balance. If there are competing priorities, there should be clear guidance from leaders on which goal or objective is more important. Ideally, it should be clear to all employees that values should not be sacrificed to achieve growth or revenue goals.

The Incentives Should Focus On Quality, Not Quantity, or at Least Not Just Quantity

Companies should choose goals that focus on the net value. Established targets should represent the amount less than the associated "costs". Leaders should focus on the profitability of a product rather than the revenue or top line. For example, there may be different behaviors driven by incentives based on gross sales versus net sales. How so, you ask? Sales representatives may push products to customers who didn't want those products simply to earn their commissions and then simply process a return for the unwanted products. There should be a focus on quality, when establishing performance metrics.

The "Carrots" and "Sticks" Should Apply to Everyone – No Exceptions

Carrots and sticks work much better when it is consistently applied to everyone. Carrots won't be as effective in motivating people once employees start to notice that it's given out discriminately. Similarly, employees won't take sticks too seriously, if they see others not being held accountable when rules are broken. This is about holding everyone accountable (more on accountability in a later chapter of the book).

Incentives Should Avoid Unintended Consequences

Incentives are not always well thought out by leaders. Many suffer from "short-termism" when establishing performance metrics. Unintended consequences may not be obvious or contemplated; however, they must be considered. This means monitoring behaviors after a new set of performance metrics have been implemented and keeping a watchful eye on red flags that may appear. Leaders should review exception reports for changes in historical trends to identify any undesirable outcomes as some outcomes may not reveal themselves immediately. If unfavorable outcomes are emerging, then leaders may need to revise their compensation structures.

Incentive Compensation Structures Should Be Reevaluated and Revised as Needed

Industries, organizations, leaders, people, and organizational goals can all change over time. It is important to have a process for reviewing, soliciting feedback, and revising the current compensation structure as needed to adapt to internal and external changes. For example, incentives that may work for one generation of workers may no longer motivate the next generation. Similarly, customer sentiment and the drivers behind consumer behavior may also change with time.

Success Case: Bridgeport Financial

What does a healthy and effective incentive compensation structure look like? One company that broke the tradition in incentive compensation methodology of its industry was Bridgeport Financial (Sinek, 2009). The debt collections industry is known to be harsh, sometimes even ruthless, in its efforts to collect from individuals and businesses who owe money. Tactics for success in collecting unpaid debt typically include some level of aggression and intimidation. In an indirect way, employees in this industry were incentivized to be this way. Their bonuses were based on how much they could collect. However, at Bridgeport Financial, employee bonuses were based not on how much they could collect, but rather on how many "thank you" cards the collection agents sent out to customers. Christina Harbridge, the owner of Bridgeport Financial, believed that the collections agents would have more success collecting if they listened to the customers' situation and treated them with respect (Sinek, 2009). The approach was to develop a rapport with the debtor and understand their financial situation in attempts to agree upon a payment plan that would work for them yet still allow Bridgeport to collect the money. How well did this approach work for the company? Bridgeport Financial collected 300% more than the industry average.

The systemic nature of the Wells Fargo account fraud is astounding. Even more shocking is how long this program was allowed to occur. According to records, employees reported the wrongdoing as early as 2005 (McLean, 2017). Based on the company's own internal analysis, these activities occurred through 2016 which means this was happening over a decade-long period. Unfortunately, the employees who tried to alert leaders using the company's ethics hotline did not get a response or recalled that "nobody seemed to care". Whatever happened, the issues reported by employees did not appear to be adequately addressed, investigated, and resolved. This is what regulators call recidivism, a term used for repeat offenders. Without accountability, there is no incentive to stop committing the crime. This leads us to the next deadly sin: lack of accountability.

Bibliography

Chris Arnold, "Former Wells Fargo Employees Describe Toxic Sales Culture, Even At HQ," *NPR*, October 4, 2016, https://www.npr.org/2016/10/04/496508361/former-wells-fargo-employees-describe-toxic-sales-culture-even-at-hq

Geoff Colvin, "Inside Wells Fargo's Plan to Fix Its Culture Post-Scandal," *Fortune*, June 11, 2017, https://fortune.com/2017/06/11/wells-fargo-scandal-culture/

Jack Kelly, "Wells Fargo Forced To Pay $3 Billion For Bank's Fake Account Scandal," *Forbes*, February 24, 2020, https://www.forbes.com/sites/jackkelly/2020/02/24/wells-fargo-forced-to-pay-3-billion-for-the-banks-fake-account-scandal/?sh=

Bethany McLean, "How Wells Fargo's Cutthroat Corporate Culture Allegedly Drove Bankers To Fraud," *Vanity Fair*, May 31, 2017, https://www.vanityfair.com/news/2017/05/wells-fargo-corporate-culture-fraud

Simon Sinek, *Start with Why*. New York: Penguin Group, 2009.

Ken Sweet, "Wells Fargo says 3.5 million accounts involved in scandal," *AP News*, August 31, 2017, https://apnews.com/article/c3de75ac78004f04be8291b1b76c2cd0

P.D. Witman (2018). Teaching Case: "What Gets Measured, Gets Managed" The Wells Fargo Account Opening Scandal. *Journal of Information Systems Education*, *29*(3), 131–138.

3
Lack of Accountability

"It is not only what we do, but also what we do not do, for which we are accountable"

– Moliere

In May 2010, as Rafael Morales Valencia stepped outside a church after his wedding ceremony, assassins invaded the courtyard and forced the wedding party to the ground. They then kidnapped the groom, his uncle, and his brother (Dart, 2012). They were transported to a safe house where they were tortured and asphyxiated with duct tape wrapped around their faces. Two months earlier, in a separate incident, Lesley Redeifs and her husband were ambushed after leaving a children's birthday party in Juarez, Mexico. Their SUV was sprayed with bullets and Lesley, who was a US consulate employee, was shot twice in the head. She was four months pregnant. Both these incidents were executed by the most brutal drug cartels in Mexico. Drug cartels need money to run their operations which means they need banking services just like any other business. The bank of choice for these drug cartels to launder their money was Hongkong and Shanghai Banking Corporation, or HSBC. The victims' families filed a suit against the bank claiming that HSBC "knowingly provided continuous and systematic material support to the cartels and their acts of terrorism by laundering billions of dollars for them".

Lessons Learned: HSBC

Former employees of HSBC described a boiler-room environment overseen by managers uninterested in investigating transactions with possible links to drug trafficking, terrorist financing, or other illegal activities (Mollenkamp & Wolf, 2012). They complained that concerns of suspicious activities were dismissed by superiors. Instead, the

DOI: 10.1201/9781003288787-3

single-minded focus was on clearing out the paperwork as fast as possible. Other former workers of the bank compared the workplace to "just a factory" with "a lot of pressure to get investigations closed". Supervisors wanted "quantity, not quality". They said these compliance efforts were more cosmetic than concrete and were told to close cases even if they seemed suspicious. HSBC was challenged with effectively monitoring trillions of dollars flowing annually through its offices in 80 countries and territories all while ensuring the money was clean.

In the days leading up to HSBC's testimony before a Senate panel over alleged anti-money laundering lapses, Stuart Gulliver, the CEO at the time, sent a message to employees communicating the following (Rushe, 2012):

> Between 2004 and 2010, our anti-money laundering controls should have been stronger and more effective, and we failed to spot and deal with unacceptable behavior. It is right that we are held accountable and that we take responsibility for fixing what went wrong.

The problem was that the bank's illegal activities didn't start only in 2004 or end in 2010. Investigations found persistent breaches in the bank's anti-money laundering compliance since then. HSBC Holdings ultimately agreed to pay $1.9 billion in forfeitures and penalties in 2012 and enter into a deferred prosecution agreement (DPA) with the US Department of Justice (DOJ) for their violations of the Bank Secrecy Act, the International Emergency Economic Powers Act, and the Trading with the Enemy Act ("HSBC Holdings and HSBC Bank USA N.A....", 2012). According to court documents, the bank had illegally and willfully failed to maintain an effective anti-money laundering (AML) program and failed to conduct due diligence on its foreign correspondent affiliates. HSBC's failure to implement proper anti-money laundering controls facilitated the laundering of hundreds of millions of dollars in drug proceeds through the US financial system. More specifically, several HSBC subsidiaries admitted to a laundry list of violations, including:

- At least $881 million of illicit proceeds from drug cartel operations was laundered through HSBC Mexico into HSBC US ("HSBC Holdings and HSBC Bank USA N.A....", 2012).

- HSBC Group's compliance department communicating to senior executives that HSBC Mexico AML function was "virtually non-existent".
- HSBC Mexico used lower risk rating to bypass stricter controls required for higher risk-rated entities, resulting in $670 billion in wire transfers going unmonitored.
- HSBC US failed to routinely and adequately monitor over $9.4 billion US dollar cash purchases resulting in suspicious activities to go undetected and unreported.
- Employees knowingly accepted illicit proceeds from Mexican drug cartels and did so for at least eight years despite such activities being known at the highest levels at HSBC Group.

As damaging as the above highlights may seem, the full details contained in court documents paint a picture that is exponentially worse than any summary could possibly provide. But there's a more shocking revelation. This is not the first time HSBC has been caught and admonished by regulators. In 2003, Federal Reserve Bank of New York regulators cited HSBC for failing to comply with AML laws. HSBC entered into an agreement to improve its procedures for identifying and preventing money laundering. That was nine years prior to the 2012 DPA agreement. HSBC had received yet another warning.

The most damning lines from the official documents about the company's culpability were the following:

- HSBC Group established AML policies at HSBC US that gave the money launderers uninhibited access to the US financial system despite their knowledge of money laundering activity ("HSBC Holdings and HSBC Bank USA N.A….", 2012).
- HSBC Group had the power to stop the known abuse of HSBC Mexico's correspondent relationship with HSBC US but allowed it to continue.

The facts presented in these court documents paint a picture of an organization that seemed to consistently not hold their employees accountable for wrongdoing or at least did not make the changes necessary to systematically change behaviors. The illegal activities continued to occur again and again. It is tempting to continue with the status quo when that status quo is profitable for the company. However, organizations must part with processes or people that do not align with their core values.

Healthy Attributes: Accountability

If lack of accountability is one of the deadly sins of organizational culture, then redemption comes in the form of the following attributes related to accountability that could be more conducive to a healthy culture:

- Organizations need to establish policies.
- Organizations need to implement processes to ensure compliance with the policies.
- Organizations need to identify and monitor exceptions.
- Organizations need to understand the reasons behind exceptions.
- Organizations need to have an effective process for resolving the exceptions.
- Organizations need to continuously improve.
- Organizations need to have consequences for breaking the rules.

Organizations Need to Establish Policies

It is not enough to have a stated mission and core values. Organizations need to interpret their values into policies. What are the rules of engagement for employees to follow? What is acceptable and what is unacceptable? Policies, as well as procedures, provide a roadmap for day-to-day operations while adhering to internal guidelines as well as compliance with external laws and regulations. If those rules are not documented, then you cannot hold people accountable to them. Some examples of policies that could be the most impactful to providing guidance on acceptable behavior for employees in the workplace include the following:

- Code of Conduct or Ethics policy
- Procurement policy

- Travel and Expense policy
- Conflict of Interest policy
- Whistleblower policy
- Workplace Health and Safety policy
- Antibribery/Corruption policy

Organizations Need to Implement Processes to Ensure Compliance with the Policies

Once the rules have been established and documented, there needs to be processes to support the employee's ability to comply with those policies. If policies are the "what", then processes are the "how". Processes can be manual or automated. They can be centralized or decentralized. The more automated and centralized the processes, the more likely the processes are consistently executed. There should be key process owners that play a critical role in ensuring compliance with standardized processes. Whatever form they take, processes and controls should facilitate an organization's ability to flag exceptions or deviations from the established rules.

Organizations Need to Identify and Monitor Exceptions

What good are policies and processes if no one monitors compliance with those policies and processes? Organizations need to implement controls and monitoring activities to detect noncompliance with company policies, procedures, or performance expectations. Such controls may take the form of recurring exception reports that flag outliers. These management reports need to be reviewed in a timely manner. Management reports are detective controls and, therefore, are backward looking. Management will be alerted to exceptions after the activity has already occurred. More proactive controls are those that alert management of certain activities in real time. Ideally, the controls are embedded in organizational systems which automatically identify and prevent exceptions from even happening. For this process to be effective, organizations need to define what an exception or outlier means. This requires leaders to define target metrics and acceptable ranges for performance outcomes.

Organizations Need to Understand the Reasons Behind Exceptions

Once it has been identified that there has been a breach in compliance with company policies or standard procedures, then there needs to be an appropriate response. To be better informed on what the right response should be, one must understand the root cause. Otherwise, companies could be addressing the symptoms rather than the causes which could lead to the problem occurring again. Below are some categories of the most common root causes:

- Lack of effective policies: employees did not know what the company rules are.
- Lack of effective procedures: employees did not know how the rules impact their day-to-day operations in their individual role and responsibility.
- Lack of effective communication: employees did not receive information about the rules in a timely or effective manner.
- Lack of effective training: employees did not understand how to practically implement the policies and procedures.
- Lack of prioritization: employees did not prioritize compliance with a rule (due to competing priorities).
- Lack of management monitoring: leaders did not prioritize their attention and focus on employees' compliance with rules (leaders were incentivized to prioritize a competing objective).
- Lack of resources: leaders did not prioritize the resources (e.g., budget, people, tools, etc.) needed to comply with the rules.

For ease of future reference, this list of common root causes can also be found in the appendix section (see Appendix VII) with some additional insightful comments.

Organizations Need to Have an Effective Process for Resolving the Exceptions

Organizations need to have resources and expertise in place to research the exceptions and understand the root causes. Once the root causes have been identified, there can be an appropriate response to resolve the exception. Policies may be outdated and need updating or they may have become altogether irrelevant. Processes and procedures need to support new systems or reorganizations of businesses or become more agile to accommodate a rapidly changing environment. Communication and collaboration methods may need to adapt to new ways of working. Training may need to be more interactive and engaging to be effective. Prioritizing objectives for the organization at the entity level as well as at the department level and individual employee level need to be aligned with the mission and values. Competing priorities need to be resolved. Employees at all levels need to be incentivized toward the same set of priorities.

Organizations Need to Continuously Improve

The organization needs to have processes in place to identify opportunities to improve and innovate. This could mean opportunities to improve policies, processes, procedures, tools, etc. The drive to continuously improve is critical for a company to be competitive and counter complacency. This assumes that leaders are willing to be introspective and recognize shortfalls. This requires discipline and humility. It requires leaders to be transparent with each other, with their employees, with their board, and other key stakeholders. Continuous improvement initiatives could come in the form of conducting self-assessments or peer reviews. It could also be in the form of internal audits or reviews from external consultants. This means they need to be committed to implementing the action items required to improve. This cannot be merely lip service or check-the-box exercises. Simply identifying areas for improvement is not enough. Time, effort, energy, focus, and money need to be invested to continue evolving and maturing.

Organizations Need to Have Consequences for Breaking the Rules

Sometimes, the problem is not with the organization's leaders. Sometimes, the problem is a rogue employee. This is where the individual accountability rubber meets the road, so to speak. If the problem is not related to an organizational shortcoming, then there must be some sort of corrective action. What if the policies and processes were in place and communicated, but the employee simply ignored the rules? Additional training may need to be administered. A warning may need to be given and documented in personnel files. Termination may also be necessary. Whatever the consequence, it needs to be consistently applied across the organization.

Success Case: McDonald's

For a successful example of holding an employee accountable for their bad behavior, McDonald's could serve as the poster child. Steve Easterbrook was promoted to the position of CEO of McDonald's in 2015 but was fired in 2018 for violation of company policy "involving a recent consensual relationship with an employee". Prior to his appointment as CEO, the company's same store sales had fallen for six straight quarters in the USA. During his four short years at the helm, he achieved 13 consecutive quarters of positive global comparative sales. There were many more successful initiatives under his tenure, including:

- Launching a McDonald's delivery service
- Expanding breakfast to be served all day
- Adding espresso-based drinks to the menu
- Remodeling of restaurants for an upgraded look
- Acquiring tech startups to help speed up drive-thru's

Despite having a goose that was laying golden eggs, McDonald's held their CEO accountable to their core values and terminated him. A day after Easterbrook was fired, the company's stock took a hit, sinking as much as 3%. McDonald's did the right thing, despite the negative impact on their stock (Climent, 2020). Dips in the stock price are, for the most part, temporary. The negative impact of not holding employees accountable for breaking company policy may not be as measurable but can be far-reaching, long-lasting and much more damaging.

Lack of accountability will only set a precedence for more bad behaviors, not only from the employee who exhibited the bad behavior but from other employees. Arguably, rules are necessary to keep employees in line. However, one could simply just hire the "right" employees, as defined by the organization, so that you wouldn't need as many rules to keep the wrong employees in line. It is all a matter of how you acquire and manage your talent. We discuss the problems of the next sin – ineffective talent management – in the next chapter.

Bibliography

"Cease and desist order against HSBC North America Holdings," *Board of Governors of the Federal Reserve System*, October 7, 2010, https://www.federalreserve.gov/newsevents/pressreleases/enforcement20101007a.htm

Shosy Climent, "McDonald's former CEO was just named in a lawsuit alleging sexual relationships with multiple employees. Here are 18 major changes he led during 4 years at the helm of the fast-food giant," *Business Insider*, August 10, 2020, https://www.businessinsider.com/mcdonalds-fired-ceo-changes-company-2019-11

Tom Dart, "Families of Americans killed by Mexican cartels sue HSBC," *The Guardian*, February 11, 2012, https://www.theguardian.com/business/2016/feb/11/families-of-americans-killed-by-mexican-cartels-sue-hsbc

"HSBC Holdings and HSBC Bank USA N.A. admit to anti-money laundering and sanctions violations, forfeit $1.256 billion in Deferred Prosecution Agreement," *United States Department of Justice*, December 11, 2012, https://www.justice.gov/opa/pr/hsbc-holdings-plc-and-hsbc-bank-usa-na-admit-anti-money-laundering-and-sanctions-violations

Carrick Mollenkamp and Brett Wolf, "HSBC's money-laundering crackdown riddled with lapses," *Reuters*, July 13, 2012, https://www.reuters.com/article/us-hsbc-compliance-delaware/special-report-hsbcs-money-laundering-crackdown-riddled-with-lapses-idCUKBRE86C18H20120713

Dominic Rushe, "HSBC chief admits bank failed to control money laundering," *The Guardian*, July 11, 2012, https://www.theguardian.com/business/2012/jul/11/hsbc-failure-control-money-laundering

4
Ineffective Talent Management

"The first method for estimating the intelligence of a ruler is to look at the men he has around him"

– Niccolo Machiavelli

At about 2:20 in the morning on January 25, 2002, Cliff Baxter drove his Mercedes Benz a mile and a half from his home in an affluent suburb of Houston (McLean & Elkind, 2003). He parked his car in the middle of the street on Palm Royale Boulevard with the doors locked and the engine still running. He then lifted a Magnum revolver to his right temple and pulled the trigger. The police found a suicide note that he left for his wife Carol. He also left behind two children. He was only 43 years old. He retired in May 2001 to spend more time with his family. Just a few months into his retirement and a few weeks before his death, he was subpoenaed by a Senate subcommittee investigating his former employer, Enron. He was one of 29 executives from the company named as defendants in a shareholder lawsuit.

Cliff was the embodiment of the American dream. He graduated from New York University and became an Air Force captain ("Enron's J Clifford Baxter: A Profile", 2002). After leaving the military, he received his MBA from Columbia University. He later worked in investment banking prior to landing a job at Enron where he quickly moved through the ranks to become the chairman and chief executive of North America as well as Chief Strategy Officer. Cliff was clearly driven and a fast-rising star – the type of talent that fit in well at Enron. Jeffrey Skilling, CEO of Enron at the time, characterized his company as the "ultimate talent company". Before Skilling was promoted to be Enron's CEO, he started the corporate division known as Enron Capital and Trade in 1990. He decided to bring in "a steady

DOI: 10.1201/9781003288787-4

stream of the very best college and MBA graduates he could find to stock the company with talent".

The Talent Myth

In an excerpt from an article titled "The Talent Myth" in *The New Yorker* magazine, Malcolm Gladwell writes about the "talent mind-set" as the new orthodoxy of American management:

> It is the intellectual justification for why such a high premium is placed on degrees from first-tier business schools, and why the compensation packages for top executives have become so lavish. In the modern corporation, the system is considered only as strong as its stars, and, in the past few years, this message has been preached by consultants and management gurus all over the world. None, however, have spread the word quite so ardently as McKinsey, and, of all its clients, one firm took the talent mindset closest to heart. It was a company where McKinsey conducted twenty separate projects, where McKinsey's billings topped ten million dollars a year, where a McKinsey director regularly attended board meetings, and where the CEO himself was a former McKinsey partner. The company, of course, was Enron.
>
> (Gladwell, 2002)

Lessons Learned: Enron

The former McKinsey and CEO of Enron was Jeffrey Skilling. Skilling had a theory: "If you hire smart people, it didn't matter whether they had any experience" (McLean & Elkind, 2003). He was known to say, "I'll take a smart, thoughtful guy who fails over a person who is successful". As we all now know, his approach to talent management may have been one of the primary reasons why things did not end well for Enron. There are countless examples of tragic mistakes to cite from the book *The Smartest Guys in the Room*, but there are also some key highlights of talent management failures at Enron.

Rick Buy

Enron had established a Risk Assessment and Control (RAC) Department because Skilling knew Wall Street wanted to see a strong system of internal controls after he was named president of the company (McLean & Elkind, 2003). The RAC department's mission was to assess every Enron deal greater than $500,000 based on the risks of the proposed transaction, thereby allowing Enron to portray itself as a company that could take on risks in an informed and responsible manner. To lead this function, Skilling picked Rick Buy as his Chief Risk Officer. Rick was a soft-spoken individual who was uncomfortable with confrontation. A former Enron executive believes that Skilling's selection of a "meek" Chief Risk Officer was no accident. When his analysts raised issues with a deal, Rick would dutifully take them up the chain of command but would ultimately cave to the company's senior traders and deal originators. There were times when frustrated RAC executives refused to sign off on a bad deal, but Rick would overrule them. It is business wisdom that many of a company's best deals are the ones it doesn't make. But it was difficult to do the right thing at Enron. The performance review process was designed to beat the RAC into submission. Traders and deal originators sat on the very panel that ranked the RAC executive who reviewed their transactions. It was a conflict of interest akin to allowing the foxes to watch the hen house.

Andy Fastow

One cannot talk about Enron's demise without bringing up the Chief Financial Officer (CFO), Andy Fastow. Once again, Enron installed the "wrong man in the wrong job for the wrong reason". Andy didn't have the knowledge required to be the CFO of a major company. Andy's experience was in corporate finance. He supposedly knew so little about accounting that some had little confidence he could even dissect a balance sheet. His skills were limited primarily to creating financial structures to allow the company to hit its financial targets. For Enron to continue to grow, they needed capital. There were only three ways to fund growth. Companies can take on debt, issue stock, or draw from their existing cash flow. But Skilling didn't like any of these options. He didn't want to take on any more debt for fear of jeopardizing its credit rating. He also didn't want to issue more stock for fear of diluting the earnings per share. As for the third option, they were short on cash. It was Fastow who created the innovative structured financing vehicles, the now infamous "Special Purpose Entities" (SPEs). These SPEs allowed the company to keep fresh debt off the books by camouflaging it as a minority interest in a joint venture in the financial statement disclosures rather than on the balance sheet. These SPEs provided Enron with around $20 billion worth of capital a year. In Fastow's first full-length interview after exiting prison, he reflects on his days at Enron with these words (Primeaux, 2016):

> ...we hired the brightest, most ambitious young people, and they were smart enough to figure out what the CFO just did...so, despite your corporate code of conduct and your code of ethics, those people saw that this guy became CFO, and he is incredibly misleading.

Compliance with actual prescribed accounting standards would not have provided Skilling with the financial numbers he wanted, so he placed a finance guy to structure financing deals that produced the desired numbers for Wall Street. That was how to get promoted at Enron. That was how talent management was done at Enron.

Jeffrey Skilling

Enron's problematic approach to talent management was not a bug, it was a feature (McLean & Elkind, 2003). Skilling had very clear ideas about how to build an organization, what to look for in people, and how those people should be rewarded. A former Enron managing director recalls Skilling telling him that "all that matters is money" and "you can buy loyalty with money". As it turns out, no company can properly operate effectively over the long term if every employee is a free agent, motivated solely by greed, no matter how smart the employees are. Before Skilling was promoted to CEO of Enron, he led the company's global finance function, which was later renamed Enron Capital and Trade Resources, or ECT. Skilling ran this division like a start-up, instituting rules and practices that were often at odds with the rest of Enron. One former employee who worked for ETC had this to say: "We had the authority to do anything and everything we wanted to do". And that is exactly what happened. For example, ETC had its own compensation system. Skilling implemented a very competitive performance evaluation system called the Performance

Review Committee (PRC). It involved bosses and colleagues providing "feedback reports" to the PRC ranking employees on a scale of 1 through 5, with 5 being the best and 1 being the worst. One former executive recalled that "what really counted was the bottom line". If the employees were making money but "being total jerks to people", they would be forgiven. Conversely, it was normal for someone to get a 5 for teamwork, but if they were a 1 in earnings, they ended up with an overall ranking of 1. If you weren't doing deals, your contribution to the company was valued at a very low level. People manipulated the system. Sometimes managers would purposely sabotage one candidate to ensure room at a higher level for one of their favorites. In the end, PRC no longer reflected a true meritocracy as intended, but rather a perversion of it. As Skilling saw it, the PRC would produce the best of Enron, but many believed it fostered the worst: ruthlessness, selfishness, and greed. The company's focus on the bottom line was driven by the fact that Enron promised its investors an aggressive earnings growth rate of 15% per year. A big incentive for achieving double-digit earnings growth was that it would make its executives rich, since a significant portion of their compensation was tied up in stock options. Such a high bar was hard to jump over consistently year after year, thereby leading Enron to resort to aggressive accounting tactics that ultimately led to their downfall. One could argue that the unspoken company mission, for all intents and purposes, was for executives and other key employees to use Enron as a vehicle to personally enrich themselves.

Imagine you are building a team of athletes to win the gold medal in the sport of rowing. If you were somehow able to put together the best rowers in the entire nation onto one team, you could almost be guaranteed to win the gold. Each of the rowers you selected has a proven record of consistently winning rowing competitions and is in the best shape of their lives. You provide the team with the best oars money can buy. But what if each of these rowers do not row together or in the same rhythm or even in the same direction? Will the boat make it to its destination or go around in circles and eventually sink?

A focus on individual motivation, performance, and loyalty could inadvertently ignore other attributes that are critical to achieving the organization's objectives collectively as an entity. These other skills include the soft skills to work in a team, the empathy to lead people, and the integrity to prioritize doing the right thing for the company's best interest over your own. The best performers who may thrive in one type of corporate culture could fail miserably in another, very different, culture.

Healthy Attributes: Talent Management

So, then what can companies do to ensure the talent they bring into their organizations will have the soft skills to work with other employees toward a common purpose, as well as be a good fit into the company's culture? How can leaders unleash all the potential of each individual employee through collaborative efforts rather than in competition against one another. If ineffective talent management is one of the deadly sins of organizational culture, then redemption comes in the form of the following attributes related to talent that could be more conducive to a healthy culture:

- Employees should know and understand the organization's overall mission.
- Employees should understand how their roles and responsibilities support the mission.
- Employees should embody the organization's values.
- Employees should be competent to perform their roles.
- Organizations should evaluate employees against the core values.
- Organizations should have an effective process for training and developing employees.
- Organizations should have an effective process for assessing employee engagement.

Employees Should Know and Understand the Organization's Overall Mission

Assuming the organization has a good mission as their north star and a set of core values to guide them, the company must develop a strategy that achieves this mission. The strategy should not be a well-kept secret shared only amongst the executive team, but rather should be communicated to and clearly understood by all employees. Although this alignment seems trivial and obvious, some organizations can certainly fall victim to leaders whose ambitions to build their kingdoms overshadow their commitment to the company's mission. The culture should emphasize prioritizing the organization's mission when there is a conflict with other objectives whether that be departmental objectives or individual goals. Everyone should be rowing toward the same destination.

Employees Should Understand How Their Roles and Responsibilities Support the Mission

It is important that all employees at all levels throughout the organization understand how their role and responsibility support the corporate strategy. This "line of sight" into how everyone's role impacts the overall strategy. No matter how small or indirectly, it is important to ensure everyone is unified in their "why". Knowing the "why" helps employees understand their purpose within the organization. For Enron, it seemed employees lost sight of any true business purpose and defaulted to the modeled behaviors of their leaders who were motivated by profits and personal gain. Leaders should connect the dots for employees by explaining how each of their individual goals plays a part in supporting the organization's overall strategy and mission.

According to popular legend, John F. Kennedy was touring NASA headquarters in 1961 when he encountered a janitor mopping the floors (King, 2019). He asked the janitor why he was working so late. The janitor replied, "Mr. President, I'm helping to put a man on the moon". Whether the story is true or not, it drives home the point that if an organization has an inspiring mission, every employee, from the astronauts to the janitors, are all united in working toward the same goal.

Employees Should Embody the Organization's Values

Once all employees understand the mission, it is equally important for them to understand the organization's values. Corporate values are the DNA of the culture. Assuming the organization has a set of core values that forges their desired culture, the challenge for all leaders is to bring talent into the organization that is not only competent but also have values that align with the corporate values. Companies have well-established talent management processes to determine competency, including job descriptions, skills tests, and the like. However, many organizations do not have effective mechanisms within their arsenal to determine whether an individual's values align with their core values. The company could build their interviewing methodology and use behavioral interview questions to identify these behaviors in prospective candidates. Human Resources departments can help hiring managers by developing value-based or behavior-based interview questions and providing training on how to conduct such types of interviews.

If a company places importance on values such as collaboration and accountability, certain questions could tease out the candidate's tendencies for collaboration or taking accountability for failures as well as prioritization of company goals over individual gains. Business reference checks could also include similar questions addressed to former employers to validate the candidate's answers. Some organizations are even incorporating personality tests into their talent acquisition process.

Employees Should Be Competent to Perform Their Roles

Although it may be too obvious to mention that employees should have the core competencies for their positions, it needs to be stated. Too many people have had to grit their teeth and be silent as they witness working with or, worse yet, reporting to individuals who land their roles based on relationships or nepotism. That is not to say that employment through relationships is mutually exclusive from being well qualified for the job. However, all too often, individuals who are not competent have attained leadership positions resulting in negative consequences reverberating throughout the organization. One of those consequences includes creating a culture where decisions are made based on relationships or loyalty rather than on what is best for accomplishing the mission.

Organizations Should Evaluate Employees against the Core Values

Equally important to assessing candidates during the recruiting process, organizations should also evaluate employees to determine whether they continue to uphold corporate values. Like the hiring process, evaluating employees has traditionally been focused on core competencies and not adherence to values. Therefore, performance metrics have also been more oriented to quantitative measures such as deliverables or work output. It can be more challenging to evaluate employees based on abstract attributes related to behaviors. However, there are questions that can be incorporated into the performance review process to determine whether employees are embodying an organization's values, including the following ("100 Examples of core values review questions"):

- To assess collaboration: does the employee make decisions with a focus on what's best for the team, not just for individual achievement?
- To assess transparency: does the employee share information openly?
- To assess teamwork: does the employee proactively offer assistance and support to their coworkers?
- To assess accountability: does the employee accept responsibility for their actions, admit mistakes, and learn from them?
- To assess adaptability: does the employee accept and use feedback from managers and coworkers to improve their performance?
- To assess communication skills: does the employee communicate and treat others with respect in all situations?
- To assess initiative: does the employee proactively seek opportunities for continuous improvement?

This is by no means a complete list, but it does provide examples of the types of questions to ask.

Organizations Should Have an Effective Process for Training and Developing Employees

Once companies have acquired their desired talent, their job is far from over. A company is responsible for the institutional support system that sets their employees up for success. It is not enough that employees know the company's mission. There are as many paths to achieve this mission as there are individuals within the company. It would not be prudent to assume everyone will achieve the mission in the manner intended by the leaders without a road map. Policies, procedures, and controls are critical to ensure employees work within the boundaries of the company's values. A company's policies embody WHAT is valued in the organization. Procedures embody HOW these values are implemented throughout the organization's day-to-day operations. Controls are the processes that prevent outliers from occurring or alert management when the policies and procedures are not being followed. Training and development further reinforce employees' understanding of policies and procedures. Leaders should invest in their most important asset with necessary training and development.

Organizations Should Have an Effective Process for Assessing Employee Engagement

Employee engagement surveys have been around for several decades now. Yet, they are still often confused with employee satisfaction surveys. Although the two have related measures, there are some differences. Employee satisfaction surveys are designed to gather opinions on HR-related issues such as bonus programs, benefits, and work–life balance ("Employee satisfaction vs. employee engagement", 2012). Employee engagement is a newer concept that attempts to assess an employee's level of commitment and connection to the organization. It is theoretically possible to have a satisfied employee with a low engagement level. For example, someone who happily puts forth the bare minimum to "get by" but is not committed to putting in extra effort to further the success of the organization's mission.

With improved engagement and connection, employers are hoping to have more productive, loyal, and committed employees. However, companies should not view engagement surveys as a "one and done" exercise. Leaders should have a process to assess engagement on a recurring basis. More importantly, organizations should be transparent with the results and have a process to address the gaps identified from the surveys. Leaders should communicate both the areas that are positive and the areas that need improvement as well as management's plans for remediation. If no action is taken to resolve grievances, then employees will eventually stop participating in such surveys.

By no means is anyone saying that Enron's one fatal flaw was related to talent management alone. There is never only one reason for corporate failures. However, one could easily make an argument that if employees are an organization's "most important asset", then failing to lead and manage this most important asset effectively may be at least one of the primary reasons the company fails. The foundational trifecta for all organizations is: people, processes, and tools. But who makes the processes and the tools? It all comes back to the people.

Success Case: Southwest Airlines

Southwest Airlines is well known for its success as it relates to talent management. The company has enjoyed a reputation for hiring people that fit their corporate culture (Weber, 2015). They receive a job application every two seconds. They hire less than 2% of all applicants. The company's approach to recruiting is to focus on alignment with the organization's core values. The following characteristics are written on their "Purpose, Vision and Promise" web page as well as on every job description (Makovsky, 2013):

- A warrior spirit (a desire to excel, act with courage, persevere, and innovate)
- A servant's heart (the ability to put others first, treat everyone with respect, and proactively serve customers)
- A fun-"luving" attitude (passion, joy, and an aversion to taking oneself too seriously)

As it turns out, hiring for values is good for business. Southwest has managed to achieve the following (Southwest Airlines Company, 2020):

- 47 straight years of profitability
- Recognized as a Best Employer in Forbes' 2019 list
- Named to Glassdoor's Best Places to Work list for the 11th consecutive year

Southwest Airline's stated values are further broken down into three different pillars (https://southwestcultureconnection.com/culture-of-southwest/):

- Me: How I show up every day?
- We: How we treat each other?
- Southwest: How Southwest succeeds?

Under each of the above three pillars are nine more specific attributes that are expected of all Southwest Airlines' employees. Not to leave these attributes up to interpretation, each of these nine attributes is described with more granularity using three bullets for each of the nine terms. For example, under "Honest", the bullets are:

- Speak up
- Be transparent
- Tell the truth

Encouraging and expecting every employee to be transparent and tell the truth seems obvious, yet some organizations are challenged with doing this very thing. We discuss the importance of transparent communication in the next chapter.

Bibliography

"100 Examples of core values review questions," *Threads Culture*, https://www.threadsculture.com/review-questions

"Employee satisfaction vs. employee engagement," *ADP Research Institute*, 2012, https://www.adp.com/~/media/ri/whitepapers/employee%20engagement%20vs%20employee%20satisfaction%20white%20paper.ashx

Enron's J Clifford Baxter: A Profile," *BBC News*, January 27, 2002, http://news.bbc.co.uk/1/hi/business/1784945.stm

Malcolm Gladwell, "The talent myth," *The New Yorker*, July 14, 2002, https://www.newyorker.com/magazine/2002/07/22/the-talent-myth

Judy King, "How great leaders communicate big vision so that others want to join in," *Medium*, November 29, 2019, https://medium.com/@Jude.M/how-great-leaders-communicate-big-vision-so-that-others-want-to-join-in-d3296e7ca37e

Ken Makovsky, "Behind the Southwest Airlines culture," *Forbes*, November 21, 2013, https://www.forbes.com/sites/kenmakovsky/2013/11/21/behind-the-southwest-airlines-culture/?sh=7a4012bc3798

Bethany McLean and Peter Elkind, *The smartest guys in the room: The amazing rise and scandalous fall of Enron*, New York: Portfolio Penguin, 2003.

Emily Primeaux, "Numbers manipulator describes Enron's descent," *Fraud Magazine*, March/April 2016, https://www.fraud-magazine.com/article.aspx?id=4294991880

Southwest Airlines Company, "Southwest Airlines reports 47th consecutive year of profitability," *PR Newswire*, January 23, 2020, https://www.prnewswire.com/news-releases/southwest-airlines-reports-47th-consecutive-year-of-profitability-300991895.html

Julie Weber, "How Southwest Airlines hires such dedicated people," *Harvard Business Review*, December 2, 2015, https://hbr.org/2015/12/how-southwest-airlines-hires-such-dedicated-people

5
Lack of Transparency

"Three things cannot be long hidden: the sun, the moon, and the truth"
– Buddha

Henry Mosley was a veteran of Silicon Valley's technology scene. In March 2006, Mosley joined Theranos as the CFO working for Elizabeth Holmes, the company's promising young founder. After Elizabeth returned from a live demonstration to Novartis in Switzerland, Mosely learned that the company's blood testing technology didn't always work. In fact, he was stunned to discover that it only appeared to work because the image on the screen showing the accurate results was a recorded result that was displayed at the end of each demo. Investors were led to believe that the results were extracted in real time from the blood placed inside the cartridge. Mosley had a weekly meeting with Elizabeth, and he decided he would bring up his concerns during the next meeting scheduled for that afternoon. He brought up the investor demos which relied on recorded results rather than real results and said "We've been fooling investors. We can't keep doing that". Elizabeth's expression suddenly changed from a cheerful demeanor to a hostile one. With a cold stare, she told Mosley "Henry, you're not a team player. I think you should leave right now". There was no mistaking that Elizabeth was not merely asking him to get out of her office, she was telling him to leave the company. Mosley had just been fired.

Lessons Learned: Theranos

Investors

Elizabeth had asked Mosley to put together some financial projections so she could show investors. After submitting the first set of numbers, she asked him to revise them upwards. He agreed to the more ambitious revenue forecasts because he thought the Theranos

DOI: 10.1201/9781003288787-5

blood-testing system worked. However, the red flags began to surface. One primary reason for the high valuation was due to the agreements that Theranos had told investors it had with pharmaceutical partners. The investor presentations listed six deals with five companies that would generate revenues of $120 million to $300 million over the next 18 months as well as another 15 deals under negotiations. The pharmaceutical companies were going to use Theranos's blood-testing system to monitor patients' response to new drugs. Mosley's unease with all these claims had grown. For one thing, in his eight months at Theranos, he had never laid eyes on any of the pharmaceutical contracts. Every time he inquired about the contracts, he was told they were "under legal review". Mosley only lasted eight short months as CFO at Theranos.

Employees

The atmosphere at Theranos' offices was described as oppressive. The head of IT deployed security features that made everyone feel they were under surveillance. You couldn't put a USB drive into an office computer without it being known. One employee who was caught doing just that was fired. To receive their severances upon termination, employees were required to sign nondisclosure and nondisparagement agreements. Employee departures, like Mosley's, weren't announced or explained. A colleague might be there one day and gone the next and colleagues would have no idea as to the reason why. In fact, the company's computer network was set up in such a way that information was split into silos hampering communication between departments and employees who couldn't even exchange instant messages with their coworkers. The chat ports were blocked. Keeping the employees in the dark was intentional. The less interaction between employees, the less they were able to compare notes and piece together the truth among themselves. Theranos operated under a culture of "secrecy and fear".

Customers/Patients

As it turned out, Elizabeth created a secretive culture because she was trying to hide the truth. Theranos blood-testing machines did not work. The idea behind the company's innovative equipment, the Edison, was to replace the traditional needle drawn blood with a finger prick to perform multiple blood tests. The problem was that the amount of blood from a finger-stick was simply not enough of a sample to run multiple blood tests. To address this, the company needed to dilute the blood from the finger-stick sample to make them bigger. When you dilute the samples, however, you lowered the concentration of analytes in the blood to a level the machine could no longer measure accurately. Inaccuracies in blood test results could produce two undesirable outcomes: false positives that could cause a patient to have an unnecessary medical procedure or a false negative that could cause a patient with a serious medical condition to go undiagnosed and untreated potentially leading to worse health outcomes or unnecessary deaths.

Board of Directors

Avie Tevanian was on Theranos' board of directors. He had worked with Steve Jobs at NeXT, the software company that Jobs created after being ousted from Apple. Jobs had brought Avie over with him when he returned to Apple in 1997 making Avie the head of software engineering. Avie was one of Jobs' oldest and closest friends. Avie noticed by the third board meeting that Elizabeth would present increasingly rosy revenue projections based on deals that were being negotiated with pharmaceutical companies. But the revenues wouldn't seem to ever materialize. There were also repeated delays with the product's rollout with the explanations changing repeatedly. If the company was in the final stages of fine-tuning the equipment, how could a completely different technical issue be the new holdup every quarter? In fact, as Avie reviewed 12 months of board materials from Theranos, he noticed a "series of irreconcilable discrepancies" in the information provided. When he tried to address his concerns with Elizabeth, she rallied powerful board members against Avie. He ultimately was asked to resign.

Theranos' downfall was deceiving everyone about their progress (or lack of progress). Innovation takes time and revolutionary products require numerous iterations of trial and error before it works. But at Theranos, the idea of "fake it till you make it" was taken to an extreme. On January 3, 2022, Elizabeth Holmes was found guilty of four fraud-related charges (Jackson, 2022). Each count carried with it a maximum 20-year prison sentence, a $250,000 fine, and a requirement to pay restitution. Not only did Holmes defraud investors, but she deceived Theranos' employees, customers, business partners, and board members.

Healthy Attributes for Transparency

If lack of transparency is one of the deadly sins of organizational culture, then redemption comes in the form following healthy attributes related to transparent communication that could be more conductive to a healthy culture:

- Communication throughout the organization should be accurate, complete, and timely as it relates to all stakeholders, including:
  - The board,
  - The CEO and executives,
  - The employees, and
  - The external stakeholders
- Communication should be free of horizontal silos across functions.
- Communication should be free of vertical silos up and down the hierarchal layers.
- Communication should be written, documented, and ratified when appropriate.

Communication to the Board

Effective communication to board members should, at a minimum, answer the following questions:

- How does the organization's strategy support the mission and vision?
- Is the strategy achievable within the set timeframe and with the current organizational capacity?
- How will the strategy impact employees, customers, and other stakeholders?

- What are the biggest challenges/risks to executing the strategy?
- What are the mitigation plans in place to address these challenges/risks?
- How effective are the mitigation plans (i.e., are the residual risks within the organization's risk appetite)?
- How effective/successful (or not) is the organization at achieving the strategy?

Communication to the CEO and Executives

The information that flows to the CEO and the executive leadership team should consider the following:

- What type of information is important?
- Why is this information important?
- Who all needs to receive this information?
- How is this information being used?
- How often is the information being reported?
- When does the information trigger some type of action from executives?
- What determines if there needs to be a change to what is reported upwards?

Communication to Employees

The information that flows to the employees should address the following questions:

- What is the organization's mission?
- How does the employee's role, goals, and objectives help to further the organization's mission?
- How will the employee's performance be measured?
- What are the organization's values (what behaviors are rewarded/punished)?
- In what areas is the company doing well?
- In what areas is the company not doing well?
- What do we need to do as a company to be better and improve?

This is by no means a complete list, but it does highlight some key points for each audience.

Communication to External Stakeholders

The most important time to ensure effective communication to external stakeholders is during a time of an organizational crisis. External stakeholders include customers, external auditors and regulators, financial institutions, and investors as well as other business partners. During a crisis event, there are key points of information that external stakeholders all want to know. The following attributes should guide their communication to their external stakeholders:

- Be transparent and timely about communicating the fact that the company has a problem.
- Take ownership of the problem.
- Provide information about the impact of the problem on the organization.
- Have an action plan for addressing and resolving the problem.
- Hold the responsible individual(s) accountable for the problem.
- Provide assurance on how the organization will be able to prevent these problems from happening again.
- Provide updates as more information becomes available.

Communication Should Be Free of Horizontal Silos across Functions

Regarding information that is communicated horizontally, this is complicated by the different leadership styles of each of the executives. Some leadership styles are driven by control of information which breeds silos. Leaders may or may not be responsible for creating silos within the organization, but they are responsible for knowing that information silos exist. Once the silos have been identified, leaders can either allow those silos to continue or encourage leaders and their respective functions to collaborate and share information. What they tolerate and don't tolerate in terms of constructive management styles will certainly signal to their deputies whether they will have a promising future at the company or, conversely, whether they are an outlier that will slowly be pushed out over time.

Communication Should Be Free of Vertical Silos across Functions

Regarding information that is communicated down to the employee base, it is a matter of removing the hierarchal silos as much as possible.

Obviously, it is neither feasible nor necessary to have everyone in the company be a part of every meeting or discussion. However, the goal should always be to push important and relevant information out as clearly and quickly as possible. The more time that passes without the right information communicated to the masses, the more likely that rumors will emerge to fill the waiting void. It should also be noted that silence can be deafening. No communication at all is also a form of communication in and of itself. In many cases, silence is almost always perceived in negative terms.

Communication Should be Written, Documented, and Ratified When Appropriate

As mentioned in a previous chapter, some things need to be written down. Important policies that underpin the rules which the organization holds dear should be in writing. Some things cannot be left up to chance or interpretation. Important policies and procedures not only need to be documented but also reviewed and formally ratified before communicating to the organization. Not only do formal policies facilitate accountability within the organization, but it also shows external stakeholders that such principles are important to the company. By clearly drawing the bright red lines, leaders are placing guardrails that help to communicate to employees the level of risk leaders are willing to accept. Policies are critical for helping leaders manage the risks to the organization.

Success Case: Zappos

If Theranos was a case study of a complete and abject failure of transparent communication, then what would be representative of the ideal environment for communication? Is there an organization that has achieved, or is pursuing with some degree of success, an organizational culture that is free of silos across as well as up and down the chain of command? Is there such a company that is designed to promote a safe space for feedback from all employees regardless of title or position?

In 2013, Tony Hsieh decided to replace Zappos' traditional organizational structure with a radical "self-governing" system called a holacracy (Groth, 2013). Instead of a traditional top-down hierarchy, a "holarchy" distributes power more evenly. There are no titles and no managers. The company will be made up of different circles – approximately 400 circles – and employees can have any number of roles within those circles. There will be people who hold a bigger scope of purpose than others, but everybody is empowered and expected to lead in their own roles. There can be no hiding under layers of titles and responsibilities. Radical transparency is the goal in which the focus is on the work, not the role.

One of Zappos' core values is "Build open and honest relationships with communication" (Corcoran, 2022). Employees who feel safe and empowered to give feedback to their superiors are more likely to offer ideas on how to improve the business, as well as identify and communicate potential threats. The company's core values are extended to its customers and vendors. They realize the importance of communication with all their partners. Seventy-five percent of their business comes from repeat customers, even though their products' prices are far from being the lowest in the market (Frei & Morriss, 2020). The company takes orders as late as midnight and delivers them to the customer's door before breakfast. If the customer doesn't like the product, they can return it for free. Customers tend to buy from companies they trust.

The same holds true for vendors. Vendors tend to work with companies they trust. The best way to earn that trust is to fully commit to transparency. The company realized that if vendors knew as much about Zappos' business as their buyers did, the company could build more trust, develop healthier relationships with vendors, and ultimately generate higher revenue and profits. Zappos created an "extranet" which allows their vendors to have complete visibility into the business, including inventory levels, sales, and profitability (Cook, 2020). If Zappos gave complete transparency into their pricing models, then vendors would know exactly how much Zappos can afford to spend on their products. The vendors started selling their products at a fair price which allowed vendors to turn a higher profit. As a result, more vendors wanted to do business with Zappos, which resulted in a better mix of products for customers. Everybody wins.

Time will tell if this unconventional model is sustainable as the company grows both in size and complexity. Adjustments to business models may be required to adapt as the company evolves, but evolution is necessary for survival of any company. What should remain constant and consistent is transparency, in whatever way companies choose to achieve it. Transparency means communicating both the good and the bad. It is necessary for all stakeholders to know both the successes and challenges of the organization. This includes the ability to identify all the risks that could impede an organization's achievement of strategy which is critical for companies to manage their risks. We discuss risk management next.

Bibliography

John Carreyrou, "*Bad blood: Secrets and lies in a Silicon Valley startup*," New York: Vintage Books, Penguin Random House, 2018.

Andy Cook, "Transparency in business: The what, why, and how," *Tettra*, April 15, 2020, https://tettra.com/article/transparency-in-business/

Michael Corcoran, "What Zappos, Google, and Bridgeater can teach us about the importance of speaking up," *NeuroLeadership Institute*, June 30, 2022, https://neuroleadership.com/your-brain-at-work/zappos-google-bridgewater-teach-about-speaking-up/

Frances Frei and Anne Morriss, "Uncommon service: The Zappos case study," *Inc*, April 25, 2020, https://www.inc.com/inc-advisor/zappos-managing-people-uncommon-service.html

Aimee Groth, "Zappos is going holacratic: no job titles, no managers, no hierarchy," *Quartz*, December 30, 2013, https://qz.com/161210/zappos-is-going-holacratic-no-job-titles-no-managers-no-hierarchy

Sarah Jackson, "Theranos founder Elizabeth Holmes has been found guilty of 4 fraud-related charges after a monthslong federal trial," *Business Insider*, January 3, 2022, https://www.businessinsider.com/elizabeth-holmes-theranos-trial-found-guilty-of-wire-fraud-conspiracy-2021-12

6

Ineffective Risk Management

"Money often costs too much"

– *Ralph Waldo Emerson*

Amber Barbosa didn't graduate college (Chris, 2009). Despite not having a college degree, she was a 28-year-old making nearly $500,000 in 2006. She was a mortgage broker at New Century Mortgage Corporation, a subprime lender. Her income allowed her to live just outside of San Francisco with a nice 27-foot Bayliner boat, several houses, a Mercedes, and a Cadillac Escalade. Her employer offered her 1 or 2% of the price of the loan as a kickback for selling higher interest rate loans to customers even if it wasn't in the customer's best interest. An even higher kickback of 3% would be paid to mortgage brokers that sold a negative-amortization loan. These loans offered low payments initially but often exploded on the homeowner as interest rates reset at much higher levels. The riskier the loan, the higher the kickback to the broker.

Anthony Narag also worked as a loan officer for several different mortgage brokerage firms. He remembered another type of high-risk loan called the "stated-income loans" which were originally designed for self-employed people with irregular income streams. During the housing boom, most people who got them weren't even self-employed. The brokers would just exaggerate the income stream to justify a big loan which was set to adjust to a high interest rate. These loans sometimes needed a supporting letter from a certified public accountant (CPA). However, an account executive once told Narag and other brokers not to worry about the letter, since he had "a CPA in [his] back pocket". Everyone involved looked the other way because "the money was so good." Narag was making $10,000 to $15,000 a month easily.

DOI: 10.1201/9781003288787-6

Another broker, Darryl Toney, stated that he was trained to give homeowners the hard sell to get them into aggressive high interest rates even if it meant convincing them to refinance instead of staying with a fixed-rate loan they could afford. After a year of working as a subprime mortgage broker, he started getting calls from his customers who could no longer afford their loans asking for help. He couldn't help them, so he eventually quit his job.

This wasn't a case of a few rogue brokers. The entire system was designed to produce this outcome. What price are companies willing to pay for the kind of money they strive to generate? This is a matter of risk taking. Stated differently, the question every leader should ask is this: how much risk should the company accept in their quest to make more money? In some cases, a company pushes the risk pedal to the floor and drives the car right off the cliff. That is the eternal dilemma for all leaders: take too little risk and you may leave opportunities on the table but take too much risk and you could put the company in hot water. The goal is to make decisions within the sweet spot (COSO Thought Leadership in ERM, Risk Assessment in Practice).

Lessons Learned: 2008 Financial Crisis

So far, the book has used examples of individual companies to represent each of the seven sins. But what if one of the sins could easily be represented by not just one company or even a multitude of companies but, indeed, an entire industry? What common thread weaves together the fall of Bear Stearns, Lehman Brothers, and hundreds of other banks whose names were less recognizable? What caused the need to bail out many other companies, including Goldman Sachs, American International Group (AIG), and Fannie Mae? The impact of the 2008 financial crisis was pervasive and colossal in nature. It has been estimated that more than 26 million Americans lost their jobs and approximately four million families have lost their homes to foreclosure (The Financial Crisis Inquiry Commission, 2011). Nearly $11 trillion in household wealth vanished.

The consequences of the 2008 financial crisis are so far reaching that many, if not most, people have experienced or at least heard of the 2008 financial crisis. Not many, however, may know about the

Financial Crisis Inquiry Commission (Commission) and the 663-page report that was produced by this Commission. This Commission was established as part of the Fraud Enforcement and Recovery Act passed by Congress and called to examine the greatest financial crisis in America since the Great Depression. During its research and investigation, the Commission reviewed millions of pages of documents, interviewed more than 700 witnesses, and held 19 days of public hearings in New York, Washington, D.C., and communities across the country. The Commission drew several insightful conclusions in their report, but two of these conclusions were especially noteworthy:

- The financial crisis was avoidable.
- Failures of corporate governance and *risk management* were a key cause of the crisis.

The Commission found in their investigation that banks systematically made loans that they knew borrowers could not afford and that these loans could cause massive losses to investors in mortgage securities. As early as September 2004, executives of well-known financial institutions recognized that many of the loans they were originating could result in "catastrophic consequences" and certain high-risk loans could result in foreclosures. But they did not stop. There was an excessive amount of borrowing and risky investments. Too many financial institutions acted recklessly, by taking on too much risk, with too little capital. In the years leading up to the crisis, many financial institutions and households borrowed at levels that made them vulnerable to financial distress. The five major investment banks in 2007 – Bear Stearns, Goldman Sachs, Lehman Brothers, Merrill Lynch, and Morgan Stanley – had leverage ratios as high as 40 to 1 (The Financial Crisis Inquiry Commission, 2011). This meant that for every $40 in assets, there was only $1 in capital to cover losses if the value of those assets dropped. Less than a 3% drop in asset values could wipe out the entire firm.

Large investment banks focused their activities increasingly on risky trading activities that produced hefty profits. These financial institutions also took on enormous exposures in acquiring and supporting prime lenders and creating, packaging, repackaging, and selling trillions of dollars in mortgage-related securities. Taking on a dangerous level of risk may not necessarily be in and of itself an organization's downfall, assuming there are effective measures in place to adequately manage the risk. Indeed, this was not the case.

But financial institutions are juggernauts in measuring financial risk, or at least they should have been. There were leading indicators that should have been warning signs. In the decade preceding the collapse, there were many signs that house prices were inflated. Lending practices had become too lax. Too many homeowners were taking on mortgages and debt they could not afford to pay. So, what happened to the risk management systems of these financial institutions?

Diving deeper into Lehman Brothers (Lehman), just one of the companies that collapsed during the financial crisis, there were many lessons to be learned. In terms of risk management, Lehman was thought to have a very respectable risk management system. Even in 2006, just two years before Lehman filed for bankruptcy, the Securities and Exchange Commission viewed the company's risk framework as being fully compliant with regulatory requirements (Wiggins & Andrew, 2014). However, beginning in late 2006, Lehman began dismantling its risk management framework in pursuit of its new growth strategy by doing the following:

- Escalated the risk appetite limits (e.g., the firm increased its risk appetite limit by a staggering 74% from 2006 to 2008) as well as increasing usage against these limits
- Disregarded numerous risk limit overages, including:
  - Concentration limits on its leveraged loan and commercial real estate business
  - Single transaction limits on leveraged loans
  - Single transaction limits in commercial real estate areas
- Excluded its riskiest positions in real estate from stress tests resulting in the company operating without a true measure of the level of risks it was assuming

To put all this in layman terms, if Lehman were a car, the guardrails were moved increasingly closer to the edge of the cliff. In addition, instances of the car driving over the guardrails were ignored. To make matters even worse, the car's dashboard metrics to warn the driver of the impending disaster were disabled.

Healthy Attributes for Risk Management

If ineffective risk management is one of the deadly sins, then leaders need to implement an effective Enterprise Risk Management (ERM) governance framework that has the following healthy attributes:

- Establish risk appetite thresholds
- Communicate the risk management process across the organization
- Define the roles and responsibilities for risk management
- Embed risk management in day-to-day operations
- Establish, track, and manage risk metrics
- Report the status of risk management activities to the board
- Adjust the risk management process as needed

Establish Risk Appetite Thresholds

The risk appetite should align with the organization's mission and values. There are inherent risks in any business across all industries. Every decision made by a leader should weigh the risks with the potential rewards. Leaders are responsible for establishing the risk appetite for their respective organizations. If the company were a car, how fast do leaders want their employees to drive the car in reaching their destination? The faster the car is driven, the sooner the destination is reached. But there are speed limits for a reason. It is tempting to push beyond the speed limits. However, the faster people drive, the more likely people could lose control of the car and the more damaging the crash would be, not only to the car itself but to the people inside the car. Leaders must balance the speed of delivering results with the risks associated with the established risk appetite. Employees need to know where the bright red lines are that should not be overstepped.

Communicate the Risk Management Process across the Organization

Although the designated risk officer, risk committee, executive team, CEO, and the board play key roles, all employees should be aware of the company's risk management policies. Policies and procedures should be established and communicated to inform employees how to navigate risks related to their specific job function. It is important to communicate and train employees about the organization's risks and how they can impact those risks in their respective roles and responsibilities.

Define Roles and Responsibilities for Risk Management

Risk management is not the responsibility of a few armchair warriors sitting in an ivory tower. Everyone in the company has a role to play. The full board should have primary responsibility for risk oversight including approval of the company's risk appetite. Management must set the risk appetite and assign owners to each risk. Risk owners are responsible for understanding, measuring, monitoring, and managing the risks to an acceptable risk tolerance level as defined by the organization. The risk officer or owner of the enterprise risk management process itself is responsible for establishing the risk management framework and methodology that the organization adopts in its efforts to identify, prioritize, and address risks. Everyone else in the organization supports the risk owners in mitigating their respective risks in their individual roles and responsibilities.

Embed Risk Management in Day-to-Day Operations

Risk management can take many forms, but it cannot be an appendage or side project to operations. To be truly effective, risk management should be embedded into operations, part and parcel to decision-making and strategy setting. Responsible risk-taking should be incorporated into the employees' job description, and goal/objective setting as well as the performance evaluation process. Imagine how different the outcomes would have been if employees within the financial services industry were evaluated based on consistent mortgage payments by their customers or keeping the number of customer defaults below a certain percentage rather than the number of mortgages that they were able to process within a given time frame.

Establish, Track, and Manage Risk Metrics

To manage anything, it must be measured. This includes managing risks. Companies measure a number of performance metrics. Most of these key performance indicators tend to be outcome metrics:

revenues, profitability, growth percentage, turnover, workplace injuries, etc. The outcome metrics are lagging indicators. They are the outcome of past performance. An effective enterprise risk management process requires that companies also measure their key risk indicators. These are leading or predictive indicators. These metrics are indicators of what the outcome will likely become. For example, the number of minor injuries that has occurred at a work site is a leading indicator of how many serious injuries may occur. The number of serious injuries that has occurred at a work site is a leading indicator of how many deaths may occur. Therefore, if you want to have an impact on decreasing the number of safety-related deaths at your company, then you should manage the leading indicators. Companies should manage the key risk indicators of an outcome that they are trying to avoid. Another example would be employee turnover. If companies are trying to avoid a high turnover rate, a leading or key risk indicator to manage may be to track and monitor the number of employee relation complaints. Management should be alarmed if employee relation complaints is trending upward. They shouldn't wait until the turnover rate ticks upward to take action. The trick is to know what the key activities or indicators are driving the undesired outcomes.

Report the Status of Risk Management Activities to the Board

Having an effective process in place to manage risks for the organization is a part of good governance. So, it is no surprise that the board, similar to management, would want and need to know about the company's efforts to manage their risks. More and more, we are seeing regular communication to the board on the status of their enterprise risk management initiative. Not only is enterprise risk management a quarterly board agenda item, but also some larger organizations have board-appointed risk committees. Boards want to know the organization's top risks, the mitigation strategies in place to address those risks, and the effectiveness of those mitigation efforts.

Adjust the Risk Management Practices as Needed

One of the mistakes that Lehman made was that their stress tests did not originally include proprietary investments because these assets had always been a small portion of their entire portfolio. However, as the company pursued its new strategy, its proprietary positions in commercial real estate investments became a greater portion of its holdings. Yet, the company failed to adjust its stress test models for these changes in its strategy. As companies evolve their strategies over time, people and processes must adapt to the changes.

A substantial strategy change could significantly impact a company's risk profile. Whether the company undergoes a merger/acquisition, expands into a new geographical region, or adds a new service line, such initiatives may introduce new risks or additional layers of complexity. Strategy changes could also cause changes in the interactions with existing risks as well as the trajectory or velocity of risks.

Success Case: Michael Burry

So many companies and people made the wrong decisions, not unlike lemmings following each other off a cliff. Was the entire financial world the victim of a lack of data to make the right decisions or was it just the wrong interpretation of available data? Was there anyone who got it right? There was indeed at least one person who drew the right conclusion based on the same set of facts and acted accordingly.

Michael Burry was doing his residency at Stanford University in California when he left school to start his own hedge fund, which he named Scion Capital (Szramiakje, 2017). He returned an impressive 55% in his first year during a period when the S&P 500 fell 12%. He credits his successful results to an investing approach called "value investing", whereby he makes all his investment decisions based on a concept of "margin of safety". The margin of safety is a principle of investing in which investors only purchase assets with market prices significantly below their intrinsic value. By buying assets at prices well below their target prices, this discounted price builds in a margin of safety in case estimates are incorrect. This conservative approach was used by Burry to manage his investment risk and it worked. In 2005, Burry used his analysis of mortgage lending practices and realized the riskiness of the subprime markets. Millions of borrowers with low income and no assets bought homes with enormous leverage and no down payments for mortgages they couldn't afford. Yet, the banking system was valued as if these mortgages were all solid. He saw the eventual collapse of the mortgage industry. Although Burry was using this margin of safety to make good decisions for investing, one could use a similar approach to help make good business decisions so that organizations can avoid taking on more risk than they can afford. In other words, organizations should establish a risk appetite that limits how much they are willing (or afford) to lose on the downside. Companies should use the concept of risk appetite to limit their potential losses when taking risks. Michael Burry's story was told in both a book and movie, "The Big Short". In short (pardon the pun), Michael Burry had the right threshold, or appetite, for the level of risk he was willing to accept.

The highest levels of leadership are responsible for establishing the risk appetite for their organizations. Everything starts and ends with the leader. Indeed, leadership is the mother of all seven sins of organizational culture. We discuss the last of the seven sins in the next chapter.

Bibliography

Arnold Chris, "Ex-subpprime brokers help troubled homemakers," *NPR*, April 9, 2009, https://www.npr.org/templates/story/story.php?storyId=89505982

COSO Thought Leadership in ERM, Risk Assessment in Practice. https://www.coso.org/Shared%20Documents/COSO-ERM-Risk-Assessment-in-Practice-Thought-Paper-October-2012.pdf

John Szramiakje, "Here's the story of one of the heroes of 'the Big Short'," *Business Insider*, May 22, 2017, https://www.businessinsider.com/michael-burry-life-story-2017-5

The Financial Crisis Inquiry Commission, "Financial Crisis Inquiry Report," January, 2011, http://fcic-static.law.stanford.edu/cdn_media/fcic-reports/fcic_final_report_full.pdf

Rosalind Wiggins and Andrew, "The Lehman Brothers bankruptcy B: risk limits and stress tests," *SSRN*, October 1, 2014, Risk Limits Metrick. https://papers.ssrn.com/sol3/papers.cfm?abstract_id=2588547

7
Ineffective Leadership

"When a clown moves into a palace, he doesn't become a king. The palace turns into a circus".

– Turkish Proverb

Every single sin related to organizational culture is a failure of leadership. The tone at the top is important because everything flows from the top. After all, leaders are responsible for:

- Determining the mission
- Defining corporate values
- Incentivizing employees to do the right things
- Holding employees accountable
- Ensuring the organization has the right talent with the right values
- Communication flow throughout the organization
- Establishing the risk appetite

It is critical to have a leader in place that not only is committed to the organization's mission (not his own self-serving mission) and embodies the values of the organization but also is effective in executing the strategy that supports the mission in a manner that effectively manages the associated risks within an acceptable threshold.

Healthy Attributes for Effective Leadership

If ineffective leadership is the mother of all the deadly sins, then the cure would be an effective leader who can impact the overall culture of the organization with the following healthy attributes of leadership:

- Leaders should believe in and be able to execute the organization's mission.
- Leaders should establish and embody the organization's values.

DOI: 10.1201/9781003288787-7

- Leaders are responsible for effective communication throughout the organization.
- Leaders are responsible for holding people accountable.
- Leaders should inspire their employees to do the right things.
- Leaders should develop a talent base whose values align with the corporate values.
- Leaders should establish the risk appetite of the organization.

Leaders Should Believe in and Be Able to Execute the Organization's Mission

An organization's mission and values are institutionalized. Leaders must serve the organization's mission, not to serve their own agenda for their personal gain. Most leaders may not have been involved with the formulation of the mission and values. It is certainly not a guarantee that all future leaders of an organization will agree with and embrace the mission and values. However, it is critical that leaders not have a separate agenda which may be different, or worse, conflict with the organization's mission and values. If leaders should ever stray from the corporate mission and ask employees to do anything that is counter to the mission or values of the organization, then the leader should be challenged.

Although it may be obvious that leaders should be competent to fulfill their duties, in many cases, organizations outgrow their leaders. Some leaders evolve with their organizations while others may either be incapable or unwilling to do so. A common example is when founder CEOs achieve their position by inventing or creating something. The company then grows exponentially, either organically or through mergers and acquisitions, or becomes a public company. A large public company requires more discipline, structure, and governance which could be unfamiliar or even uncomfortably restrictive to the entrepreneurial spirit. It has often been said that "what got you here, won't get you there". In fact, a recent study found that 52% of CEO departures from the companies on the Russell 3000 Index were under pressure to do so (Sahadi, 2019). Researchers found that the leading reason for the dismissal of CEOs was poor performance. Just like any other position, CEOs can also fail at their jobs. They can also underperform or make fatal mistakes.

Wells Fargo had a noble mission and vision which was to "assist customers for their financial success", yet these CEOs failed in the pursuit of their company's missions ("*Wells Fargo mission and vision statement analysis*"). In the case of Theranos, not only was Elizabeth Holmes guilty of deception but, first and foremost, she was simply not able to deliver the product that she had promised to her investors and customers. This innovative product was at the heart of Theranos' mission. If raising money was the company's mission, she would have been very successful.

Leaders Should Establish and Embody the Organization's Values

As previously discussed, it's a simple task to establish a list of core values. That's the easy part. However, a leader should not only establish the organization's values but also exhibit those values. In other words, leaders should "walk the talk". This is part of "tone at the top". Yet, there have been plenty of headlines exposing executives' extramarital affairs with employees or abusing the company's expense account. In other cases, CEOs have been accused of sexual harassment and preying on their own employees. American Apparel's founder, Dov Charney, was sued by multiple employees for sexual harassment and had to pay millions to settle the cases (Taylor, 2017). In interviews, Charney stated that "sleeping with people you work with is unavoidable". Clearly, he didn't believe in the company's most basic of values. In another case, the leaders at Uber were not able to embed their core values into their culture. Uber's stated values promote "safety for everyone" as well as "do the right thing" (https://www.uber.com/us/en/careers/values/). Despite these values, a federal investigation found that the company fostered a culture of sexual harassment and retaliation against individuals who complained about such harassment (Guynn, 2019). The company ultimately agreed to establish a $4.4 million fund for the victims. Whether leaders intend to lead by example or not, the cause and effect is unavoidable: employees will observe what you do, not what you say, and will follow your lead accordingly.

Leaders Are Responsible for Effective Communication throughout the Organization

Leaders set the tone for how much information flows up, down, and across the organization. Depending on the personalities and cultures of the board, the CEO may have a lot or not much influence about what makes it on the board's agenda. However, the CEO certainly has unwritten rules over how much detail gets presented to the board. CEOs typically review board materials before they are presented and how the original materials are edited is certainly a clue into the organization's culture of communication. Effective communication is a critical component of transparency. If employees are not aware of defects within the organization or cannot voice and escalate them, how could the organization even begin to fix those problems? Leaders cannot possibly resolve all issues on their own. They need to be honest with themselves and their employees on areas where the organization is weak. Self-introspection is necessary for continuous improvement. It is also important to realize that, without transparency, there can be no accountability. How can leaders hold anyone accountable if there is not a consistent process for identifying and communicating both failures and successes?

Leaders Are Responsible for Holding People Accountable

Company values should ultimately lead to accountability. All managers with employees reporting to them are responsible for holding their employees accountable. However, the top leaders of the organization are responsible for establishing effective processes that facilitate accountability. This includes developing policies and procedures so that employees know what the rules are. It is also the leaders who are responsible for establishing management monitoring processes to know when employees are not following the rules. When employees break rules, it is ultimately up to leaders to impose consequences including termination. Employees will certainly notice if leaders are lax with handing out penalties for noncompliance with policies. Sometimes, the root cause is not a rogue employee, but rather the entire system supported by the company itself. If the problem is pervasive, then leaders must make the necessary changes to the process so that the ship is back on the right course.

HSBC's values state that they "take responsibility" and commit to "holding [themselves] accountable" for their actions (https://www.hsbc.com/who-we-are/purpose-values-and-strategy/our-values). The company had nearly a decade to clean up its act, yet it continued to break the same laws. Interviews with the bank's former compliance officers revealed that they tried to do their jobs in monitoring suspicious activities but were ignored or rebuffed (Woodman, 2020). Some organizations put policies and processes in place to check a compliance box, but it is form over substance. The leaders bear the burden of holding employees accountable for doing their jobs. This means taking action to correct employee behaviors that are inconsistent with corporate values, even if it means terminating employees who are popular or laying golden eggs up to and including the CEO.

Leaders Should Inspire Their Employees to Do the Right Things

There are many ways leaders can inspire their employees. They can do so with their grand vision giving their employees a purpose that they believe is worth pursuing. They can inspire them with rewards that motivate them to spend their time and effort working for one organization over another. Such rewards could take many forms, including compensation, benefits, and other perks of the workplace. It could also take the form of further investment in the employee's professional development, whether their future career lies with the same organization or not. Ideally, inspiration to stay loyal to one organization could include all the above forms. Whatever way leaders choose to inspire their employees, the hope is for leaders to motivate employees to do the right things in the right way. Doing the "right things" means having a mission that has an overall positive impact on not just their customers or shareholders, but for all stakeholders, including the planet. Doing those things in the "right way" means executing in such a way that is ethical and within the confines of the law. Leaders should not use greed or deception and false hope to incentivize employees, as were the cases with WorldCom, Wells Fargo, and Theranos.

Leaders should establish performance management systems that not only assess employees based on their ability to perform their duties, but also their commitment to working within the company's rules and in conformance with organizational value systems. Leaders are responsible for developing incentive programs that motivate the right, or wrong, employee behaviors. Leaders prove through example which behaviors are rewarded and promoted versus which behaviors are discouraged and punished. Employees that do not exhibit behaviors consistent with the organizational values will eventually be pushed out or left on their own, thereby reinforcing the remaining like-minded people. It bears repeating: people will behave exactly the way you motivate them to behave.

Leaders Should Develop a Talent Base Whose Values Align with the Corporate Values

If leaders only hire talent based on core competencies, they should have a team that can execute the organizational mission. If the mission is the north star for the organization's purpose, then values are the guiding light for the organization's soul. Do you really want employees to achieve the mission using any means necessary? How do companies ensure that employees embody the values that they espouse? Although leaders cannot have a hand in hiring every employee, they are responsible for identifying and communicating the organization's core values to existing employees. They are also responsible for developing the process by which talent is acquired which hopefully includes communicating these values to prospective candidates. The vetting process for hiring employees should consider questions posed to candidates that provide insights for hiring managers to determine whether the candidates' values align with the corporate values.

Leaders are also responsible for weeding out employees who do not consistently behave and act in accordance with the corporate values. This assumes that the performance management process includes evaluation criteria for employees exhibiting those values. Again, leaders are responsible for developing the performance management process and holding employees accountable to the agreed-upon expectations, not just for performance but also behavior. Finally, leaders are responsible for ensuring there is a succession plan in anticipation of the day when the leader must pass the baton to a successor. This means that leaders should know when it is time to step down from the role.

Leaders Should Establish the Risk Appetite for the Organization

Leaders are responsible for setting goals and objectives for employees. Those goals and objectives for the organization will be as aggressive as the leader's risk appetite. There are inherent risks in any business across all industries. Every decision made by a leader weighs the risks with the potential rewards. Leaders are also responsible for establishing the risk appetite for their respective organizations.

Employees need to know where the bright red lines are that should not be overstepped. Leaders are responsible for drawing those bright red lines. They are also the ones that can move those lines or make exceptions for employees that do cross the line. How those lines are moved and when exceptions are made will set the tone for what is acceptable. Often, there are conflicts in balancing the achievement of organizational goals and the level of risk leaders are willing to accept on behalf of the organization. Leaders are tasked with making those decisions and determining the balance of priorities: staying within an acceptable risk tolerance or achieving targets.

Since leadership is responsible for corporate governance, they are responsible for the design and effectiveness of all the elements of governance. This includes the mission, values, people, communication, and processes. Every decision and action taken by leadership shapes the culture of the company. Leadership and culture are intertwined.

Throughout the book, there was at least one organization that was used as an example of each of the seven sins. The leaders of each of those entities suffered from at least one of these flaws. Some of those organizations survived and some have not because of those fatal mistakes. What would be the outcome if one leader embodied all the seven sins? What if this leader:

- Did not believe in or care about upholding the organization's mission, values, or institutional norms?
- Was motivated only to use the power of his or her position for personal financial gains?
- Never took ownership or accountability for his or her actions or the outcomes of those actions (or lack of action)?
- Hired people based on loyalty to him or her rather than on competencies or alignment with organizational values?
- Was not transparent or, worse yet, consistently has issues with facts and the truth?
- Made decisions based on furthering their personal agenda instead of consideration of the risks associated with taking certain actions (or not taking certain actions)?

- Lacked many or all the characteristics of an effective leader, including empathy, humility, and diplomacy?

One can only hope such an individual would never be placed in the highest positions of power in any organization, whether that be in publicly traded companies, private industry, nonprofit organizations, or even within government entities. Imagine the chaos that would ensue. The decisions made without consideration of the core values. The corruption that would go unchecked. The incompetence permeating throughout every level and function. The uncalculated risks that would be taken without mitigation. The damage done to all those impacted without accountability or consequence.

Bibliography

Jessica Guynn, "Uber agrees to pay $4.4 million to settle EOC sexual harassment and retaliation probe," *USA Today*, December 19, 2019, https://www.usatoday.com/story/tech/2019/12/18/uber-sexual-harassment-investigation-me-too/2694091001/

Jeanne Sahadi, "Up to half of exiting CEOs don't quit. They get fired," *CNN*, July 19, 2019, https://www.cnn.com/2019/07/19/success/ceos-getting-fired/index.html

Kate Taylor, "American Apparel's founder says that 'sleeping with people you work witih is unavoidable'," *Business Insider*, September 11, 2017, https://www.businessinsider.com/american-apparel-founder-dov-charney-on-sleeping-with-coworkers-2017-9

"*Wells Fargo mission and vision statement analysis*," https://mission-statement.com/wells-fargo/

Spencer Woodman, "HSBC moved vast sums of dirty money after paying record laundering fine," *International Consortium of Investigative Journalists*, September 21, 2020, https://www.icij.org/investigations/fincen-files/hsbc-moved-vast-sums-of-dirty-money-after-paying-record-laundering-fine/

8
Assessment of Culture

"A measure of such things which in any degree falls short of the whole truth is not fair measure"

– Plato

It is difficult to measure something like culture. However, the drivers of culture can be measured. There are many drivers of organizational culture. This book addresses several key drivers of culture. Some of those drivers, or components, have subcomponents that can interplay and interact with one another. Some components can be assessed based on its own as a stand-alone element. Other components should be evaluated in relation to other components with which there are strong interdependencies. Some components are more difficult to measure than others. This is an exercise in measuring multiple pulse points to paint an overall holistic picture of the health of the organization's culture. It's more directional, rather than an exact science.

Organizational Culture: Key Indicators

Throughout the book, there are attributes indicative of a healthy culture for each respective area discussed in each chapter. The more "healthy attributes" a company has in place with respect to all the key drivers of culture, the better the health of the organization's culture tends to be. As with anything else, many things in life are not binary. Few things in life are about choosing between only two designations: black or white or good or bad. There are shades to just about everything. The health of an organization's culture is largely driven by the maturity of the processes that are the key drivers of the culture. When assessing an organization's culture, one could be measuring the maturity of certain processes as well as tracking and monitoring the metrics of certain key indicators. The following are some recommended examples of such indicators:

DOI: 10.1201/9781003288787-8

- Organizational culture assessment
- Policy management maturity
- Process maturity
- Talent management metrics
- Industry peers
- Other external feedback
- Enterprise risk management (ERM) process maturity

Organizational Culture Assessment

The level of engagement of the collective workforce can be measured using an engagement survey. Such a survey can incorporate questions specific to the drivers of organizational culture resulting in a survey that not only assesses the employee's level of engagement, but also how the employee is experiencing the organization's culture through their perspective. As to be expected, questions between the two could overlap. Some examples of questions to include in an organizational culture assessment can be found in Appendix IV.

Policy Maturity Management

Mature policy management is a critical part of corporate governance and operations. Executives and the board should lead policy management. Rules in the form of written policies and procedures are necessary to hold employees accountable. The more mature the organization's governance over policies and procedures, the higher the probability that employees have a clear roadmap of the rules of the organization, more specifically, what is acceptable and what is not. Policies help guide expected behavior within the organization.

Organizations can measure the maturity level of their policy management system to provide a roadmap for increasing their level of maturity and optimizing their policy governance. The following policy management maturity model illustrates five stages of policy maturity (GRC 20/20 Policy Management Maturity):

- Ad Hoc
- Fragmented
- Defined

- Integrated
- Agile

Ad Hoc Organizations at the ad hoc stage of policy management maturity have reactive approaches to policy management at the department level. Businesses at this stage do not actively manage policies; few if any resources are allocated to policy management. The department addresses policy management in a reactive mode – writing policies when forced to do so. There is no ownership or monitoring of policies, and certainly no integration of policy information and processes in the context of objectives, strategy, performance, and business change.

Fragmented The fragmented stage sees departments with some structure and focus on policy management within respective functions, but they are disconnected and not working together. Information and processes are highly redundant, manual, and lack integration. With siloed approaches to policy management, the organization is still very document centric. Processes are manual and they lack standardization, making it hard to manage policies in a way that is efficient, effective, and agile.

Defined The defined stage suggests that the organization has some areas of policy management that are managed well at a department level, but lack integration to address policy management across departments. Organizations in the defined stage will have defined processes for policy management in some departments or business functions, but there is no consistency. Policy management processes have the beginning of an integrated information architecture supported by technology and ongoing reporting. Accountability and oversight for certain policy domains are beginning to emerge.

Integrated In the integrated stage, the organization has a cross-department strategy for managing policies across departments and functions. Policy management is aligned across several departments to provide consistent strategies, frameworks, templates, and processes supported by common policy information and technology. The organization addresses policy management through shared processes and information that achieve greater efficiency and effectiveness.

Agile At the agile maturity stage, the organization has completely moved to an integrated approach to policy management across the business that includes collaborative policy authoring and leveraging intelligence/cognitive technologies for regulatory change and policy mapping. There are consistent core policy management processes in place that span the entire organization and its geographies. The organization benefits from consistent, relevant, and harmonized processes for policy management with minimal overhead.

Process Maturity Model

Once organizations have developed their policies, the processes are then implemented in the form of standard operating procedures to support and comply with those policies. The processes within each organization can also have varying degrees of maturity. By measuring the maturity level of an organization's processes, one can have an additional reference point for assessing the health of an entity's culture. The more mature the organization's processes, the stronger the guardrails to prevent and detect exceptions or outliers that are indicative of rogue behavior. The "Process Maturity Model", which was adapted from the Process Capabilities Matrix published by Paul J. Sobel in 2007, has the following maturity stages (Process Maturity Model, 2007):

- Ad Hoc
- Repeatable
- Defined
- Managed
- Optimized

Ad Hoc A process that is at the "Ad Hoc" maturity stage has the following characteristics:

- No formal procedures.
- Controls are nonexistent or primarily in reaction to a "surprise".

- There are no metrics or performance monitoring.
- There are no discernable mechanisms to identify opportunities to improve the process.

Repeatable A process that is at the "Repeatable" maturity stage has the following characteristics:

- Some standard procedures exist but there is more reliance on "tribal knowledge".
- Controls in place are mostly detective controls and there are minimal preventative controls as well as being manual (not automated).
- There are few performance metrics in place, thus performance monitoring is inconsistent or informal.
- Improvement mechanisms are likely in reaction to audits or service disruptions.

Defined A process that is at the "Defined" maturity stage has the following characteristics:

- Procedures are well documented, but not kept current to reflect changing business needs.
- Preventative and detective controls are employed, but there is still reliance on manual activities.
- Some metrics are used, but performance monitoring is still manual and/or infrequent.
- Improvement mechanisms generally occur during periodic policy and procedure renewal which may only happen annually.

Managed A process that is at the "Managed" maturity stage has the following characteristics:

- Procedures and controls are well documented and kept current.
- Preventative and detective controls are employed with greater use of automation to reduce human error.

- Many metrics are used with a blend of automated and manual performance monitoring.
- Best practices and/or benchmarking are used to improve processes.

Optimized A process that is at the "Optimized" maturity stage has the following characteristics:

- Processes and controls are continuously reviewed and improved.
- Preventative and detective controls are highly automated to reduce human error and cost of operations.
- Comprehensive and defined performance metrics exist with extensive automated performance monitoring.
- Extensive best practices and benchmarking and/or self-assessment initiatives are used to continuously improve processes.

Talent Management

There are numerous talent management–related metrics that could be indicative of the health of the organization's culture. After all, if employees are a company's most important assets, then there should be metrics to measure the performance and vitality of that asset. The following are some key indicators to assess whether your employees are thriving in your organization' culture or heading for exit.

- Employee engagement survey
- Employee relation complaints
- Performance appraisal scores
- Turnover rate
- Exit interviews
- Training
- Ethics Hotline

Employee Engagement Surveys

Employee engagement surveys, not to be confused with an organizational culture assessment, could be an effective indicator of how engaged the workforce is. Many companies conduct these surveys on a recurring basis, but not everyone does it right. It is critical to ensure that the surveys are conducted in a manner to provide anonymity for the employees. If someone in the HR function is the one interviewing employees, this won't provide assurance of anonymity. The results of the engagement survey should be communicated to everyone in the organization. It is also crucial for organizations to ensure management acts on the results if there are areas where the company may be "failing".

Employee Relation Complaints

Long before an employee chooses to resign from their employer, one of the leading indicators to monitor is the number and nature of complaints that end up at Human Resource's (HR) doorstep. If employees are not getting along with one another or having issues with their managers, HR is one of the first avenues that is utilized to resolve conflicts. If there is a rising trend in the number of employee relation complaints, especially within the same departments, then there is likely a dysfunctional environment that is at the root of the problem. Even more informative is if the turnover trends can be linked with the employee relation complaints. It is obviously much less disruptive and expensive for the organization to address and resolve employee issues as they arise before it escalates into departures or, worse, legal liabilities.

Performance Appraisal Scores

Reviewing performance appraisal scores can say a lot about the employee but can also say a lot about the manager or leader. Reviewing the trends of scores can suggest a number of things, including whether the recruiting process is effective (or not), the onboarding or training programs are effective (or not), and the goals are achievable (or not). Reviewing performance appraisal scores over a certain time period could be an indicator of whether a manager is an effective leader. If the scores for the same individual have changed from a superstar to an under-performer over a short period of time, this could be an indication that the environment has impacted their performance. If there has been a change in leaders, a change in scores for the same employees could also be telling. In any case, reviewing trends in performance appraisal scores should be evaluated in conjunction with other metrics, including employee engagement, turnover rate, and training spend. Employing a 360-degree approach is recommended as it provides a more holistic assessment by incorporating multiple perspectives.

Turnover Rate

The most common metric used by companies to gauge success, or failure, of their talent management efforts is the turnover rate. Companies should not just calculate one overall rate, but rather break down the rate into voluntary versus involuntary, by department or by manager, and the turnover trends over time, including quarter to quarter and year to year. If the turnover rates or retention rates are worsening over time, this could be a clear indication of a toxic culture. If the high turnover rate is isolated to a specific department or manager, this should be investigated and resolved with that leader. All things being equal, people tend to leave their managers, not their company.

Exit Interviews

If an organization has a high turnover rate, the answer to why employees are leaving in droves could be gleaned from the exit interview. The answers from departing employees may not be as explicit as "the toxic culture", but other reasons cited are implicit of an unhealthy work environment. Some of these reasons include "poor leadership", "not feeling valued", "feeling disengaged", "overstressed", or "lack of trust". Feedback regarding the corporate culture from former employees cannot be ignored. HR functions should also pay attention to common themes and trends when it relates to exit interviews. If there is a recurring theme, there should be actionable items to address the issues with the hopes of correcting the root causes. Unfortunately, this source of feedback is dependent on employees responding. If employees are not choosing to respond, then no news is not necessarily good news. Many people understandably do not want to "burn bridges" or face post-employment retaliation from their former employers. They may prefer to play it safe with the philosophy of "when you don't have anything good to say, don't say anything at all". It would be prudent for employers to not only track trends but also the percentage of exit interview responses. Even the lack of participation in exit interviews could be indicative of an environment that does not foster trust or promote an environment in which employees feel safe to be truthful.

Learning and Development

A number that is very easy to measure is the amount of money that leaders are willing to spend on training and developing their most important asset – their people. How much are organizations willing to invest in Learning & Development (L&D) initiatives for their employees? If this is the area that gets the first cut during lean economic times, this would suggest how much, or how little, the leaders are committed to investing in their employees. As the world evolves into a more digitized workplace, upskilling employees to prepare them for the future becomes even more important. Another related metric is the number of internal promotions (versus external hires) for vacant positions. If there is adequate investment in professional development and succession planning, then the number of internal promotions should be higher, which also improves the retention rate and reduces the cost of talent acquisition.

Ethics Hotline

When employees voice their concerns through an anonymous hotline rather than having real conversations with their leaders, this suggests that they do not feel safe to speak up. It does not speak well of the culture of the organization when employees are fearful of retaliation. What types of calls are being reported into the company's Ethics Hotline from employees? Is there a theme among the employee calls? How quickly are the allegations being resolved? Are management action items to address substantiated allegations appropriate and sufficient? Are star performers being given a pass for bad behaviors? By reviewing the trends of the ethics hotline, leaders can look for potential root causes which can then be addressed. If leaders do not adequately address the issues from ethics hotline, then employees will eventually lose faith in the ethics hotline process and in their leaders.

Industry Peers

Organizations can compare just about any internal metric to their industry peers. In addition to comparing the more typical revenue and expenses metrics, there is a plethora of other metrics that can be used to evaluate against peers. The following are just a few key metrics that could provide insightful measures for organizations to compare with their competitors.

Revenues compared to competitors are a standard metric for industry benchmarking. However, if the growth rates supporting those revenue numbers are off the charts compared to peers, the question then becomes whether the rate of growth is sustainable and healthy for the organization. The case of Wells Fargo is an example where the organization's expectations of eight accounts per customer when the industry benchmark was 2.7 proved to be unrealistic and, as it turned out, fraudulent.

Revenues and growth are not the only important metrics for organizations to measure. It is, after all, the employees who can make or break the company's success. Therefore, talent management metrics should be included in the key metrics to compare to industry benchmarks, including turnover. Companies should compare leading indicators for talent management, including investment in learning and development initiatives to determine if they are keeping up with the rate at which competitors are investing in their talent. Another talent management metric that would also be indicative of how competitive the organization is in attracting talent into the organization is the compensation and benefits as compared to peers in the industry. If the company is a leader in its compensation and benefits offerings, this would also be helpful for its employee retention. Finally, comparing the number of layoffs an organization has had to initiate compared to their peers within the same industry could be an indication of how well the company is being managed in terms of long-term strategic planning or the effectiveness of their risk management process.

Within the spectrum of risk management, there are numerous risk-related metrics that can be used to benchmark against industry peers. Depending on the industry, organizations could also use risk metrics related to environmental and safety risks for the energy industry or liquidity and leverage ratios or other financial ratios for the banking industry.

Comparing these risk metrics against competitors could provide leaders with an idea of whether they may be taking on too much risk.

An organization may not be sufficiently investing in its research and development (R&D) initiatives. This is especially true if companies are offering a product in a highly competitive industry. In this age of fast-moving technological advances, companies do not want to be complacent in innovation. One of the best and easiest ways to measure the rate of innovation inside a company is to compare the amount of money invested in R&D compared to their competitors. This would include the investments in the talent of their respective R&D departments. No company wants to lose its customer base to a newer and cooler product. No one wants to be the next Blockbuster.

Other External Feedback

At the risk of drinking our own Kool-Aid, it is always a good idea to look outside of the organization for feedback. Such feedback could come from multiple sources, including:

- Customers
- Former Employees
- External Auditors
- Consultants
- Vendors
- Recruiters
- General Public

Customers

Many companies measure their worth based on the number of customers they have compared to their competitors. This is a leading indicator to the outcome indicator of customer attrition rates which can also be compared to industry peers. Although comparing metrics to peers is important, what these customers are saying about your company is probably even more important. In order to find out the "why" behind the numbers, organizations should seek honest and candid external feedback from all different sources, including what the customers are saying about the company.

Lack of discipline could result in not delivering products or services to customers in a timely manner or not meeting service-level agreements. Unless the company providing that product or service is the only game in town, customers have few reasons to remain loyal to companies that cannot meet their expectations. Metrics to measure and monitor any downward trend in customer satisfaction survey results could be a leading indicator of customer retention.

Former Employees

Feedback from former employees need not only come in the form of exit interviews. Former employees often keep in touch with their former colleagues. Individuals with whom the former employee had a good working relationship at the company may be able to solicit more candid responses after some time has passed.

Glassdoor is an anonymous online forum where former employees can rank their experience working with their former employers. Obviously, there can be some comments on Glassdoor from former employees that are fueled by vengeance so one must review the comments with a grain of salt. However, if most of the feedback is negative, then the input is no longer an outlier but a trend and should not be ignored or dismissed. If an organization consistently receives a low rating on Glassdoor and the comments reference similar issues or same departments and/or managers, it may be time to take those comments seriously. There should be a process in place to parse out the outliers and identify common themes and trends with the intent to identify the root causes and address them.

External Auditors

For public companies, the external auditors report to the Audit Committee and, therefore, in theory, are independent and objective. In addition to ensuring that a company's financial statements are complete and accurate, external auditors would be an excellent sounding board. Public accounting firms typically have an extensive list of clients, and the engagement teams are generally grouped by industry. Therefore, a company's auditors have significant insight into how mature an organization's governance processes are compared to other organizations in the same industry or of similar size, as well as how healthy the culture is compared to their other clients. After all, auditors are required to conduct their own risk assessment of prospective clients to ensure they do not take on high-risk clients. Therefore, their input could be rather insightful.

Consultants

Similar to external auditors, consultants hired to fix problems for companies have a wealth of information simply due to the fact that they solve problems for numerous other companies for a living. Companies are not paying hundreds of dollars per hour for management consultants unless they have serious issues that need solving, problems they could not solve on their own. There could be similar challenges which are somehow addressed more successfully by one company than other companies. What are those more successful companies doing differently? More importantly, what do the unsuccessful companies have in common? What lessons can be learned from other companies who have already suffered through the same problems and were successful at solving them?

Vendors

Can vendors fire their customers? They certainly can. If vendors start to slowly back away and stop participating in a company's requests for quotes and proposals, they may just be overwhelmed with other clients or this may be an indication that you are a problematic customer. The reasons could range from too many late payments or too many last-minute changes. Unexpected emergencies are understandable but when chaos is the standard and not the exception, this could eventually wear on suppliers. When operational dysfunctionality seems to be the modus operandi, it almost always means the root of the problem stems from lack of discipline or ineffective leadership which are all drivers of an unhealthy culture.

Recruiters

One specific vendor that deserves its own category are recruiters. Assuming a recruiter has a long-term working relationship with a company, they will be able to keep a pulse on how attractive a company is to candidates as well as the reputation that the company has on "the street". A recent research study shows that 77% of job seekers take organizational culture into consideration when applying for their next job ("New Survey: Company mission & culture matter more than compensation," 2019). Job seekers talk to their recruiters. Recruiters talk among themselves. Job seekers talk to their network about each other's experience with employers, past and present. This fact has only become exponentially more pervasive due to social media. Most recruiters will be hesitant to work with clients that churn and burn their employees. Companies should pay attention to the rate of job offers not accepted by candidates and have discussions with the recruiters for the reasons. Candidates are more likely to be candid with recruiters about why they chose not to accept the offer.

General Public

The court of public opinion can be rather damning to organizations. Not only can many consumers collectively decide to vote with their wallets by refusing to buy an organization's goods or services, but they can also apply pressure on other key stakeholders to "cancel" the organization by withdrawing their business or ending their partnerships. These can be polarizing times with plenty of triggering social and political topics such as climate change and racial as well as gender equality. Even people who are not consumers can have an impact if the company's actions or decisions are unpopular. A public protest in front of corporate headquarters with media coverage could certainly make a negative impact on the company's reputation within its community very quickly.

Social media has made it very easy for the public to organize and stand behind a common cause that unites large numbers of individuals with a common goal. Most organizations cannot exist without some form of social media presence which means that they need people, processes, and tools to monitor and manage the communication and real-time interactions. Artificial intelligence tools can track key words and identify patterns within mentions of the company name across multiple social media platforms and notify the organization before things escalate to a full-blown public relations crisis.

Risk Management

There are several Enterprise Risk Management (ERM) frameworks available for organizations to adopt and implement. Several notable ERM frameworks include the Committee of Sponsoring Organizations (COSO), International Organization for Standardization (ISO) 31000, and the Organization for Economic Co-operation and Development (OECD). The COSO's ERM framework has five components (Enterprise Risk Management Maturity Model OECD, 2021):

- Governance
- Strategy and Objective Setting
- Risk Culture
- Performance
    - Risk Identification
    - Risk Analysis and Evaluation
    - Risk Treatment
- Review and Revision
- Information, Communication, and Reporting

The OECD also has a robust maturity model for ranking the maturity of each of these components into five different maturity levels:

- Emerging
- Progressing
- Established
- Leading
- Aspirational

Needless to say, the more mature an organization's risk management process, the healthier the organizational culture. A more thorough description of attributes for each category can be found in Appendix III.

All the different metrics discussed in this chapter can be measured by using a general scale of either meeting a desired or target metric or expected level, falling below that level or exceeding that level. The different levels could be similar to a "grade" on a "report card". The typical red, yellow, and green traffic light colors can be used to visually display whether an organization has favorable or unfavorable results. After assessing your organization on the criteria from the list of recommended attributes, you can see a holistic picture of the health of the organization's culture. A sample of a Culture Wellness "report card" can be found in Appendix V.

What does your wellness report card look like? Are there more greens than reds? Are there more yellows and reds than you would like to see? For those of you who are not happy with your organization's current grades on the culture wellness report card, you may be asking: how does one go about systematically changing the culture? We explore this topic next.

Bibliography

Enterprise Risk Management Maturity Model OECD, 2021 https://www.gerenciandoriscosemprojetos.com/wp-content/uploads/2021/06/OCDE-2021-enterprise-risk-management-maturity-model.pdf

GRC 20/20 Policy Management Maturity, https://grc2020.com/about/

"New Survey: Company mission & culture matter more than compensation," *GlassDoor Team*, July 10, 2019, https://www.glassdoor.com/employers/blog/mission-culture-survey/

Process Maturity Model "Adapted from the Processes Capabilities Matrix", by Paul Sobel, 2007, https://www.auditboard.com/download/Process-Maturity-Model-Template.pdf

9

Culture Transformation

It is not the strongest nor the most intelligent of species that survives but the one that is most adaptable to change

– Charles Darwin

On August 6, 1997, a Boeing 747 from Korean Air began its descent toward Guam. The captain, who had flown into Guam from Kimpo airport eight times previously and was familiar with the airport and the surrounding terrain, decided to make a visual approach. It was raining. The first officer was looking for the runway, but he couldn't see it. The plane's Ground Proximity Warning System called out to indicate that the plane was only 500 feet from the ground. According to flight records, at the 1:42 and 19 second mark, the first officer suggested that they pull up and try the landing again – this is what is referred to as a "missed approach". At 1:42 and 20 seconds, the first officer repeated his suggestion, "Not in sight, missed approach". Two seconds later, the flight engineer also suggested that they "go around", but it was too late by then. At 1:42 and 26 seconds, the plane hit the side of a hill and slammed into a rocky ground at 100 miles per hour. After skidding for 2000 feet, it fell into a ravine and burst into flames. Of the 254 people who were on board, 228 lost their lives on that day.

Lessons Learned: Korean Air

Twenty years before the crash of Flight 801, a Korean Air Boeing 707 was shot down by a Soviet military jet as it wandered into the Russian airspace. Two years after that tragic event, another Korean Air Boeing 747 crashed in Seoul. Three years after that, another Korean Air Boeing 747 was lost near Russia followed by a Boeing 707 that went down over the Andaman Sea in 1987. Then, two more crashes happened in 1989 in Tripoli and Seoul followed by yet another crash in 1994 in Cheju, South Korea. For perspective, the loss rate for

DOI: 10.1201/9781003288787-9

United Airlines during the period 1988 to 1998 was .27 per million departures. If you were to compare this rate to Korean Air's loss rate of 4.79 per million departures, it is more than 17 times higher than United Airlines' loss rate for the same period.

As if these crashes weren't devastating enough, they had a near-fatal domino effect on the company. Korean Air's flight safety record had such a poor reputation that both Delta Air Lines and Air France suspended their partnerships with Korean Air in 1999. Even the US Army no longer allowed its personnel from flying with the airline despite maintaining thousands of troops in South Korea. The US Federal Aviation Administration even downgraded Korean Air's safety rating. Based on a study conducted by the National Transportation Safety Board, a typical accident involves seven consecutive human errors. These seven errors are rarely the result of knowledge or skills but rather are invariably errors of teamwork and communication.

Korean Air decided to find out what was causing their frequent crashes. In 2002, they brought in David Greenberg, an outsider from Delta Air Lines, to run their flight operations. Greenberg found that the Korean Air pilots were trapped in roles dictated by their country's cultural legacy. To put this in perspective, a study was conducted by a Dutch psychologist named Geert Hofstede in the 1960s and 1970s. Hofstede analyzed the ways in which cultures differ from one another along the spectrum of different dimensions called "Hofstede's Dimensions", which are now widely used in cross-cultural psychology. One of Hofstede's dimensions is what he called the "Power Distance Index", or PDI, which refers to people's attitudes toward hierarchy and how much a particular culture respects authority. A high PDI score indicates that a society accepts an unequal hierarchical distribution of power and that people understand their place in the system. Because the Korean culture was based on hierarchy, pilots were too deferential to their superiors to challenge them, including in the cockpit, when they have a need to speak up assertively to the captain (Kaufman, 2013). According to the *Journal of Cross-Cultural Psychology* published in 2000, the five countries with the highest pilot PDI scores were Brazil, South Korea, Morocco, Mexico, and the Philippines – in that order. South Korea's PDI score was second only to Brazil. It is probably not a coincidence that the ranking of countries with the greatest number of plane crashes by country matched up very closely with the countries with the top five highest PDI scores.

To be clear, Greenberg was not trying to change Korea's culture. He was only trying to change Korean Air's culture. Greenberg's first step was to focus on communication. His second step was to focus on training by bringing in a Western firm – a subsidiary of Boeing called Alteon – to take over the company's training and instruction program. He introduced rigorous new training and testing standards to change the "cockpit culture". He also began basing promotions and transfers on merit rather than connections and friendships. Over the course of two years, these efforts paid off to rehabilitate the airline's reputation (Kirck, 2002). Delta and Air France both approved the resumption of their membership in their code-sharing alliance. In addition, the US Department of Defense lifted a ban on its employees' flying on Korean Air's planes. Changing the organizational culture is possible. It takes time and discipline, but it can be done.

I have seen plenty of toxic cultures in workplaces as both an external auditor, an internal auditor, and a consultant. Have I ever seen a leader be successful at changing the culture? I have only seen this happen once in my 30-year career. There are entire shelves of books written about how to change corporate culture. This book is not trying to earn a place on that shelf. However, I feel compelled to devote at least one last chapter to this topic.

Success Case: The Company

I would like to share what I believe are the key initiatives that need to be implemented to change the culture. The lessons learned have been derived from several successful cultural transformations which I had the privilege of witnessing. Here are the steps taken by several leaders, who had the best of intentions to change the culture of their respective organizations (the Company) by creating an environment that would unleash the best in all its employees:

- To change the culture, you must start by changing the leader.
- Define the values of the desired culture.
- Communicate values and set expectations.
- Identify the gaps between the current and desired culture.

- Develop and implement an action plan for closing the gaps.
- Embed values into performance evaluation and hiring process.
- To maintain the desired culture, continue to assess, and implement actions as needed.

To Change the Culture, You Must Start by Changing the Leader

It may seem drastic, but it is absolutely necessary. Remember from Chapter 7 that ineffective leadership is the mother of all the sins of a toxic culture. So, the cure then is to make a change to that leadership. This applies to changing the culture of a department or function. It could apply to changing the culture of a business unit or the entire organization. Most, if not all, leaders who have attained a certain level or position in their careers are already set in their ways. The people leading departments, business units, or entire companies are typically not in their formative younger years but are usually seasoned professionals. Their values, ability to inspire others, philosophy on how best to incentivize people, the type of people they want on their team, inclination to be transparent, propensity to hold themselves or others accountable, and appetite for responsible risk-taking – these all have pretty much been baked at this point in their life. It's one thing to change a process and ask employees to change their tasks or activities. It's quite another thing altogether when you are asking someone to change their personality, their belief system, and the way they think and feel about the world.

The board may mandate that the leader change their ways, and the leader can fake it for a period of time, but you can't fake your way through a forced transformation forever. It's simply not sustainable. The new leader must be that catalyst for change. They must genuinely want and believe in the change. Changing the leader won't guarantee that the culture will successfully change. However, not changing the leader will guarantee that any attempt to change the culture will ultimately fail.

Many of the successors are external to the organization to ensure the new leader was not "tainted" by the legacy culture. It is possible to be successful with an internal candidate. However, there is a greater likelihood of success if the internal candidate is the one who is initiating and driving the change. This new leader is in the unique position to define what the new culture for the organization will be. This newly promoted CEO of the Company initiated the cultural change because he saw an opportunity to use culture as an asset to take the organization to the next level.

Define the Values Desired by the Culture

Defining the desired culture is really about identifying the values to which everyone should commit themselves and expect from everyone else in the organization. Because everyone will be held accountable for upholding these values, everyone should have a vote on what these values should be. The most common mistake that leaders make in crafting a list of values for everyone in the organization is not including everyone in the process. I have seen values developed by a few top executives behind closed doors. Upon emerging from their ivory tower, they dictate and mandate the values upon everyone else without any input from the other 99% of employees who are expected to live by these values.

What I experienced at the Company was a deliberate and methodical process whereby input was solicited from all employees using well-thought-out survey questions that were designed to determine what type of work environment would bring out the best in the greatest number of people. Through this process, common themes would inevitably surface. The raw data would produce a multitude of different words each representing the wishes of people from the trenches and on the front lines and all the way up the chain to heads of departments and senior leadership. The initial long list of words would then be consolidated and calibrated down to a short list of terms representing values. Some companies have as few as six while others may have as many as 12. This Company decided upon eight values.

Whatever number of values an organization chooses to have and whatever process is employed, the input should come from across all functions as well as from up and down the hierarchy. Representation is critical. It is important to not disenfranchise the employees from the process. If they are not engaged in the process, they will not have ownership of the results nor be committed to upholding the values.

Communicate Values and Set Expectations

Communicating anything can take so many different forms. The rookie mistake version of communicating values is to simply pay for the words to be painted on the walls or printed on banners that are then displayed throughout the office buildings. Leaders can "check the box" and say it's done, so they can move on to "more important things". I have seen this done in this way at multiple companies. It's a quick and easy way to "communicate" values. Unfortunately, it's not very effective. Below is a list of all the different methods to more effectively communicate the organization's values:

- Describe what the values represent
- Provide examples of each value in action
- Reference the values in written communication
- Reference the values in meetings
- Recognize employees who embody the values
- Communicate values to candidates
- Communicate values on the company's website

This Company took every opportunity to communicate its eight values in every way that could be communicated effectively. Similar to Southwest Airlines, this Company had succinct bullets to describe each value. The short, bulleted phrases used verbs to provide meaning in the form of action.

In addition, the communications department wrote a playbook that addressed each value in much more detail. It provided employees with examples of different scenarios and how to respond to each case in a way that is consistent with these values in the context of typical challenges an employee may encounter in their day-to-day. This playbook brought to life the practical application of the values and made it more "real world".

The CEO would write about one of the values in regular recurring email communications to all employees. It was one more touchpoint to drive home the message and, hopefully, minimize misinterpretation of each of the values. The messages were additional clarification of what each value represents as well as what the values did not represent. The values were displayed on computer monitors and seen by every employee as they walked down the halls to get from one office or meeting to another.

Employees at the Company didn't just read about the values but also heard them on an almost daily basis. Values were consistently referenced in meetings, both formal and informal. They were discussed by all ranks of the organization, not just leaders. They were used for guidance in making decisions, for generating ideas, and for determining the best ways to execute on those ideas. The values were used to call out individuals and hold them accountable if someone's behavior strayed from those values. Implementing the values of this new and improved culture was not a project, but part and parcel to how everyone conducted themselves every day in both spoken words and in action. And it was everyone's responsibility because everyone had been involved in developing these values.

The Company also publicly recognized employees who had displayed one or more of the values in executing their duties in some exceptional way. These employees were formally recognized in company emails, at company-wide employee luncheons, and at award ceremonies. Employees were also recognized during informal occasions including leadership meetings, department meetings, and cross-functional team meetings. Employees were recognized in big and small ways, with trophies and treats.

Leaders hired people with values consistent with the organization's values. I didn't find out about the Company's values once I became an employee. I first learned about the values during the interview process while I was merely a candidate for the job. Communicating the values to the candidate can be a discussion during the interview or formally written into the job description. By incorporating the values into the recruiting process, the Company tried to vet and weed out those individuals who were deemed to be a bad cultural fit. You can avoid the difficult task of pulling weeds out of your garden by simply not planting them in the first place.

Finally, the Company's values were not a well-kept secret. These values were proudly displayed on their website, as they should be. The public should know these values. Customers deserve to know the values of the Company from which they are buying. Vendors and partners should know the values of the Company with whom they have close working relationships. After all, as discussed in an earlier chapter, there is no accountability without transparency.

Identify the Gaps between the Current and Desired Cultures

Once everyone is on the same page in terms of understanding the expectations of living the desired culture, it is now possible for everyone to be vigilant in identifying the exceptions to that culture. At the Company, there would be meetings scheduled with the specific purpose of filtering out the areas where the organization was struggling the most in realizing its values. Once again, this process involved all employees. Each department would have a session to discuss their issues openly and candidly. The notes from each department session would be discussed during a leadership meeting held with all department leaders.

Develop and Implement an Action Plan for Closing the Gaps

Once a list of problematic areas have been identified and documented, the leadership group would vote on the priority of each of the issues. Through a democratic process, the top issues were prioritized. For each of the top issues, an action plan was formulated to address the root causes. The action plans need to have people assigned to execute the tasks related to each plan. There should be a governance process for monitoring progress. There should be milestones and target dates for completing action items. Success should be defined.

Embed Values into the Performance Evaluation and Hiring Processes

The values were embedded in the performance evaluations as a significant part of each employee's ranking. In doing so, the message was clear that you couldn't receive a stellar score on your evaluation just based on performance and achieving goals alone, but also on your behavior at work. Are you transparent? Do you treat others with respect? Are you collaborative? Do you hold yourself and those you lead accountable? How you achieve your goals also mattered. Incorporating the values into the employee performance evaluation allows for accountability as well as provides employees with incentives to adhere to these values.

To Maintain the Desired Culture, Continue to Assess and Implement Actions as Needed

This is a journey that never ends. It's not a destination. There is no "one and done". The desired culture for an organization is a garden that needs continual tending. Employee engagement surveys were administered every two years. In addition to engagement surveys, the Company also established an Employee Steering Committee that comprised representatives from each department in the organization. This was yet another way for the Company to keep its pulse on its employees. It was also another way to engage employees and give them a vote on the activities, events, or other initiatives they believed would help continuously improve engagement with employees. This information was communicated to the leadership team and addressed as necessary. Rinse and repeat.

It remains to be seen how well the Company will be able to maintain its desired culture. It will take collective discipline, effort, time, and energy with the understanding that the results won't be immediate or even directly traced to the bottom line. It is understood that the alternative is not a place that employees want to settle for and no longer accept.

Bibliography

Malcolm Gladwell, "*Outliers: The story of success*," New York: Brown and Company, 2008.

Wendy Kaufman, "After Aisana Crash, pilot training gets new scrutiny," *NPR*, July 9, 2013, https://www.npr.org/2013/07/09/200401572/after-asiana-crash-pilot-training-gets-new-scrutiny

Don Kirck, "New Standards mean Korean Air is coming off many 'shun' lists," *New York Times*, March 26, 2002, https://www.nytimes.com/2002/03/26/business/new-standards-mean-korean-air-is-coming-off-many-shun-lists.html

Afterword

These are all simple concepts. Isn't it just good governance? And yet, why did so many companies fail and continue to fail at these simple things? And by "fail", I mean that some of the companies discussed in the book no longer exist. Some have managed to recover, but only after incurring substantial cost. The costs incurred are not just in terms of dollars and reputation, but also in human lives. The simple answer is that, although the ideas are not complicated, it's the *execution* that's hard. What's even harder than execution? *Consistent* execution. Let's look at an example that everyone can understand – the human endeavor to lose unwanted and excess weight. The formula for losing weight is extremely simple to understand. It really is a matter of simple math: calories in minus calories out. If you consistently have a caloric deficit, you will eventually lose weight. Yet, so many people try and fail, despite doctors telling us that our health greatly depends on it, even our very lives in some cases. Again, the concept is simple, but the execution is hard. Many people can diet and exercise for a day or a week or even a month. But try being disciplined enough to do something different every day for the rest of your life. It's not easy. The people who succeed are only able to do so by building it into their lifestyle. It simply becomes a part of how they live their life. For companies, it cannot be just a project that starts and then ends. It must be embedded in the way they do business every day. The organization's culture is the foundation. If the foundation of a house is not strong, then it won't matter how nice and expensive the house is. The cracks will start to show along the walls. The doors will start to stick and not close properly. If the foundation is not repaired, the cracks will only get worse.

Some of you may be fortunate enough to consider your organization to be perfectly healthy and functional. That's fantastic. But understand that you are in very small minority. Also, be aware that leaders come and go. The next CEO through the door may change the culture, intentionally or unintentionally, and it may not be for the better. A number of things can happen to offset the balance of the

DOI: 10.1201/9781003288787-10

universe resulting in paradise lost. What's important is that people are aware and vigilant in recognizing the signs of culture decay. Culture change never happens overnight. It is a slow transformation. If organizations are trying to change a dysfunctional culture into a better one, knowing the journey is a marathon and not a sprint could certainly be discouraging. But if organizations currently enjoy a healthy culture that start to show early signs of corroding, slow change is good news because there is a fair amount of time to act. Once the red flags are noticed (see red flags in Appendix II), people need to have the courage and conviction to speak up. You should evaluate the culture that surrounds you. Is this the work environment in which you will thrive or languish? Do the core values of the organization align with your values? How many red flags would it take for the culture to be unacceptable for you?

This is about so much more than a way to make the work environment "more enjoyable" at work, although this is a noble and worthy endeavor. Remember all of the dysfunctional cultures that resulted in thousands of people to lose their jobs and livelihoods or millions to lose their homes or, in the worst-case scenario, innocent people meeting their untimely and violent death. If we could improve the health of the organizational culture and harness it to become an asset, rather than a liability, just imagine the possibilities. Indeed, it has been proven that the right culture can improve the bottom lines for companies. These are certainly not mutually exclusive of one another.

The hope is that we can all play a part, no matter how small, in our respective roles and corners of the world. Doing nothing makes one a part of the problem. Doing nothing is complacent at best and complicit at worst. Be a part of the change for better.

Appendix I
Healthy Culture Attributes

Mission:

- An organization's mission is universal or at least implicitly inclusive of all stakeholders.
- An organization's mission states what it is they do that makes the world a better place.
- An organization's mission has goals that are external to the entity.
- An organization's mission should be formally documented.
- An organization's mission should be communicated to all employees and stakeholders.
- An organization's strategy should support its mission.
- An organization's strategy should be achievable within the boundaries of its values.

Incentives:

- Incentive compensation structures should align with organizational values.
- Incentive compensation structures should establish target goals that are achievable.
- Incentive compensation structures should be risk-adjusted.

- Incentives should focus on quality, not quantity, or at least not just quantity.
- The "carrots" and "sticks" should apply to everyone – no exceptions.
- Incentives should avoid unintended consequences.
- Incentive compensation structures should be reevaluated and revised as needed.

Accountability:

- Organizations need to establish policies.
- Organizations need to implement processes to ensure compliance to the policies.
- Organizations need to identify and monitor exceptions.
- Organizations need to have an effective process for resolving the exceptions.
- Organizations need to understand the reasons behind exceptions.
- Organizations need to continuously improve.
- Organizations need to have consequences for breaking the rules.

Communication:

- Communication throughout the organization should be accurate, complete, and timely as it relates to all stakeholders, including:
  - The board
  - The CEO and executives
  - The employees
  - The external stakeholders
- Communication throughout the organization should be free of vertical silos up and down the hierarchal layers.
- Communication throughout the organization should be free of horizontal silos across functions.
- Communication should be written, documented, and ratified when appropriate.

Talent Management:

- Employees should know and understand the organization's overall mission.

- Employees should understand how their role and responsibilities support the mission.
- Employees should embody the organization's values.
- Employees should be competent to perform their roles.
- Organizations should evaluate employees against the core values.
- Organizations should have an effective process for training and developing employees.
- Organizations should have an effective process for assessing employee engagement.

Risk Management:

- Risk appetite thresholds should be established.
- Risk management processes should be communicated across the organization.
- Roles and responsibilities for risk management should be clearly defined.
- Risk management should be embedded in day-to-day operations.
- Risk metrics should be established, tracked, and managed.
- Risk management should be reported to the board on a regular basis.
- Risk management processes should be adjusted with the organization's changing strategy.

Leadership:

- Leaders should believe in and be able to execute the organization's mission.
- Leaders should establish, embody, and promote the organization's values.
- Leaders should establish the risk appetite for the organization.
- Leaders should develop a talent base whose values align with the corporate values.
- Leaders should hold everyone accountable.
- Leaders should inspire their employees to do the right things.
- Leaders are responsible for effective communication throughout the organization.

Appendix II
Culture Red Flags

To further aid in assessing an organization's culture, there are a list of red flags to look for in each of the key areas that drive culture. If you are seeing and experiencing multiple red flags across many of these areas, there is a strong probability that your organization's culture is dysfunctional. As a reminder, this is not an all-inclusive list. This list is to provide yet another reference point.

Mission/Values – Red Flags:

- The organization's mission is not inclusive of all stakeholders impacted by the organization.
- The organization's mission is focused mostly on stock price, revenue, profits, or growth.
- There is a lack of stated or documented core values.
- The organization's mission is not well communicated to and/or understood by all employees and stakeholders.
- The organization's core values are not well communicated to and/or understood by all employees and stakeholders.
- The organization's strategy does not support the mission.
- The organization's strategy is achieved in a manner that is not consistent with their core values.

Performance Management and Compensation – Red Flags:

- Incentives are based solely (or mostly) on achieving share price, revenue, profit, and/or growth goals.
- Incentives do not include consideration for achieving goals ethically, safely, legally, environmentally responsible, etc.
- Failures are opportunities to blame rather than to learn and improve.
- Incentive structure are producing unintended consequences that negatively impact the organization.
- The performance management process solicits input from managers but does not include input from peers and subordinates.
- Performance evaluations do not consider or incorporate assessment of employee's consistent adherence to organizational core values.
- Performance objectives are significantly outside of peer benchmarks.

Accountability – Red Flags:

- There are few formal or written policies and procedures in place.
- Policies and procedures are in place, but they are not updated.
- Employees are not aware of key policies and/or procedures.
- Employees do not always understand how certain policies and/or procedures impact their role.
- Exceptions and outliers are ignored or not prioritized and ultimately not effectively resolved.
- High performers are given a pass for bad behaviors.
- Leaders prioritize achievement of profits over adherence to core values.

Communication/Transparency – Red Flags:

- There is a tendency to shoot the messenger or the bearer of bad news.
- There is fear of retaliation for speaking up or challenging leaders.
- There are silos in communication across the organization.

- There are silos in communication between levels of the hierarchy of the organization.
- There is pressure to filter information depending on the audience.
- There is a tendency for hidden agendas rather than open and transparent communication with positive intent.
- There is a tendency to avoid difficult conversations rather than constructively resolve conflicts.

Talent Management – Red Flags:

- There is high turnover in comparison to industry peers.
- Learning and development for employees is not well funded.
- Training is focused on technical skills rather than soft skills or leadership skills.
- Employee career development is driven more by relationships rather than competency.
- The number of employee relation complaints is consistently high.
- The talent acquisition process does not consider alignment with core values.
- There is not an effective process for assessing employee engagement on a regular basis or for addressing issues identified in engagement survey results.

Risk Management – Red Flags:

- The CEO or executive management team does not support or is not engaged in the enterprise risk management initiative.
- Enterprise risk management is not discussed or is not a regular agenda item at board meetings.
- Enterprise risk management is treated as a project and not embedded into day-to-day operations or decision-making.
- Enterprise risk management is not aligned with the organization's strategy.
- There is a lack of enterprise risk management training or awareness for employees.
- The organization's risk appetite is not well-defined, understood, or communicated.

- There is a lack of metrics to measure risk tolerance, risk triggers, and key risk indicators.

Leadership – Red Flags:

- Leaders are not committed to the organization's mission.
- Leaders do not embody the organization's core values.
- Leaders do not hold employees accountable for their actions or lack of action.
- Leaders do not take responsibility for the organization's failures and the failures of the people they lead.
- Leaders do not share information openly or transparently.
- Leaders hire people for loyalty rather than competency or commitment to the organization's mission.
- Leaders set goals that are too aggressive (not in line with industry peers) for the organization.

Appendix III
OECD ERM Maturity

ERM Governance Maturity:

EMERGING	PROGRESSING	ESTABLISHED	LEADING	ASPIRATIONAL
The governance structure for ERM is somewhat unclear and generally uncoordinated between governance bodies.	The administration governance structure considers ERM and exists with some exchange of information between governance bodies and periodic reporting to the Executive Management Team on major risks and risk management actions.	An administration-wide governance structure is responsible for the periodic review and monitoring of key elements of enterprise risk and performance as well as setting general risk appetite.	An administration-wide governance structure regularly reviews enterprise risk and performance administration-wide and approves risk appetite and risk tolerance for major risks.	An administration-wide governance body engages in proactive and, as necessary, real-time decision-making related to risk and performance to achieve the administration strategies and objectives (including supporting objectives of other government agencies).
Levels of authority and roles and responsibilities are not well documented, understood, or applied consistently across the administration. There is consequently little review and monitoring of many risks and accountability for risk management is unclear.	Levels of authority and roles and responsibilities in some business areas are defined and documented with a focus on reviewing and monitoring major risks and performance indicators. Individual responsibilities as regards to other risks will often not be clear and risk appetite may vary widely across business units.	An operating structure is in place that sets out both levels of authority and individual roles and responsibilities that are consistently applied within most business units.	A comprehensive operating structure is in place to ensure full cooperation between governance bodies. Levels of authority and explicit roles within and across business units are clearly mapped out in operating plans and individual objectives.	The administration has well-defined and well-understood delineated roles, responsibilities, delegations of authority, and governance structures. These are regularly evaluated by management, including through periodic independent reviews, to determine if they are applied correctly or if changes are needed in the light of changing circumstances.

Source: Enterprise Risk Management Maturity Model OECD 2021.

ERM Strategy and Objective Maturity:

EMERGING	PROGRESSING	ESTABLISHED	LEADING	ASPIRATIONAL
Administration strategy and objective setting usually involve adjustments to the previous period's strategy/ objectives in the light of experience and is generally backward looking as regards to risks (i.e., with a greater focus on previously realized risks rather than an analysis of how future risks might impact the delivery of the administration's strategy). There is limited consideration of the internal and external environments and stakeholders. There is limited understanding of risk appetite by senior leadership.	Administration strategy and objective setting involves some analysis of potential delivery risks, although this may not be done in a joined-up and systematic process. Some aspects of the internal and external environment and stakeholders are considered. There is a basic understanding of risk appetite but is not yet interconnected with strategy.	When administration strategy is being developed, consideration is given to the potential effects of major changes in the internal and external environments (such as changes to government policy). Adjustments are made as appropriate in accordance with the administration's general risk appetite. This process is supported by structured inputs from business units, risk management experts, and governance committees. A risk appetite statement, that considers trade-offs, is in place and communicated appropriately.	Administration strategy is informed by comprehensive horizon scanning and scenario planning involving a wide range of internal and external stakeholders. The detailed objectives for achieving the strategy are adjusted as appropriate in accordance with the administration's different risk appetites and risk tolerances in specific areas. Risk appetite statements are articulated for key areas of administration risk. Risk appetite statements are reviewed periodically by the administration's governance structure in the light of events and appropriate adjustments considered.	The strategic planning process is supported by the use of advanced analytics using a wide range of inputs to forecast different scenarios and their impacts on the achievement of the strategy. This is done on a continuous basis allowing real-time adjustments to strategy, objectives, and/or performance measures, including changing risk appetites and risk tolerances of the administration. Risk appetite statements are incorporated into all business objectives and monitored in real-time through advance analytic techniques with suggestions for changes put forward.

Source: Enterprise Risk Management Maturity Model OECD 2021.

ERM Risk Culture Maturity:

EMERGING	PROGRESSING	ESTABLISHED	LEADING	ASPIRATIONAL
There is a general appreciation at senior level of high-level business risks, but risk management is not promoted across the administration as a proactive tool and often issues are only addressed after risks materialize.	Administration strategy and objective setting involves some analysis of potential delivery risks although this may not be done in a joined-up and systematic process. Some aspects of the internal and external environment and stakeholders are considered.	The importance of effective and joined-up ERM across all aspects of the administration is stressed by senior leadership and generally reflected in training material, performance management processes, including reporting and monitoring, and management objectives.	A strong ERM culture is visibly encouraged, supported through ongoing structured professional training, and rewarded in performance management processes. This is reinforced by consistent messaging and management behaviors.	ERM is fully integrated into core administration professional values and is reflected in day-to-day behaviors and an organizational culture focused on innovation. It is supported through a multifaceted approach for continuous training and development.
The application of ERM in general largely depends on the expertise and risk appetite of individual managers with high variability across the administration. A number of basic training courses are available although not always on a regular basis and most training is done on the job.	In-house risk management expertise exists (which may be centralized or embedded in high-risk areas). Some core training can be provided on a reactive basis for those directly accountable for identified high risk projects or issues. ERM in practice may be highly variable across the administration and often undocumented.	Risk-informed decision-making by managers is encouraged and supported, including through the provision of general guidance and assistance on demand from risk professionals. Periodic reviews are done as to the ERM culture within the administration.	There are well-communicated expectations as regards to the incorporation of ERM in decision-making at all levels as well as the involvement of risk management professionals. ERM culture is periodically measured against key performance indicators and qualitative assessments and benchmarked with other organizations.	There is real-time monitoring of behaviors and decisions to ensure alignment with core values and risk appetites, including through the use of automated and embedded advanced technology tools and techniques. This also allows the administration to make well informed dynamic changes in risk appetites and processes to respond to environmental changes.

Source: Enterprise Risk Management Maturity Model OECD 2021.

ERM Performance – Risk Identification Maturity:

EMERGING	PROGRESSING	ESTABLISHED	LEADING	Aspirational
Outside of major projects, the extent and nature of risk identification and reporting is generally left to the individual managers and business units leading to many risks not being identified other than at a very general level.	While there are standardized reporting requirements for identifying risks, the process for identifying and describing risks and for considering interrelated risks will differ across business units and will be of varying quality.	The main risks to achieving objectives are identified at regular, established intervals using a standardized process (including enterprise and business unit levels). The level of granularity of risk identification will vary across the administration. Links between different areas are often considered but this is generally done independently by business units and not subject to cross-administration review.	Risks are identified and validated consistently and in a standardized manner at each level of the administration taking into account lessons learned from prior events.	A wide range of internal and external information sources are used to proactively identify and centrally validate risks to objectives at all levels of the administration using advanced tools such as data analytics, artificial intelligence, etc.
The Executive Management Team may sometimes commission risk assessments to be done. This will largely be on a reactive basis where some risks have already materialized and in those cases will be about damage limitation than prevention or mitigation.	Risk identification is integrated into certain activities of business units considered to be of higher risk. In other areas the types of risk to be considered are left to business units resulting in variability in the quality of risk identification.	A portfolio view of risks to objectives agreed by the governance bodies exists at the enterprise level, including a risk profile for each level of the organization which is reflected in business unit plans and objectives.	Risk identification is integrated into normal day-to-day operations and this information is supplemented by periodic cross-administration risk identification activities to ensure completeness and accuracy.	New, emerging, or changing risks are proactively identified on a real-time basis including changing risk appetites and changes in the interrelation of risks across business areas.
Where risks are identified they are not consistently logged centrally or shared making it difficult to consider interrelated risks or to get a coherent or consistent picture of enterprise risks.	The high-level risks identified by the individual business units are reflected at an enterprise level after approval by the appropriate governance bodies. The governance bodies will identify and feedback some common themes and major interrelations between risks for business unit management consideration.		Enterprise risk identification includes the consideration of risks from across the units and how they interrelate and is done in a joined-up process by the governance bodies and cascaded across the administration for inclusion in plans at all levels.	Identified risks and interrelations are subject to regular peer review and challenge at all levels of the administration and fully integrated into administration wide objectives.

Source: Enterprise Risk Management Maturity Model OECD 2021.

ERM Performance – Risk Analysis and Evaluation Maturity:

EMERGING	PROGRESSING	ESTABLISHED	LEADING	ASPIRATIONAL
Risks are either not analyzed formally or risk analysis is done in an inconsistent manner based on the previous experience and management judgment and without any common format, resulting in an unreliable assessment of enterprise level risk.	Risk analysis is standardized but fairly basic in form, relying on largely subjective and broad-brush judgments which can vary considerably between business units and depend heavily on the engagement of management. There is some analysis for high-level risks that span business units on high-profile projects.	Standardized quantitative risk analysis techniques are increasingly used where appropriate to supplement qualitative analysis in a broadly consistent manner across the administration. There is increasing use of scenario analysis and/or simulations in high-risk areas to test and improve the quality and reliability of risk analysis.	Quantitative approaches are increasingly used to gain actionable insights into risks. Scenario analysis and simulations are used on a consistent and regular basis. Triggers are identified and deployed to detect a need for risk reassessment and to mitigate for potential biases in assessments.	Risk analysis is carried out using an integrated risk-assessment system based on a wide range of real-time qualitative and quantitative data, both internal and external, and using advanced technology tools (such as artificial intelligence) to map cause and effect relationships, including the impacts of interrelated risks.
Risks are largely prioritized on the basis of high-profile/high-budget projects which attract significant reputational risks. Most business areas assume a "business as usual" approach.	A broad measure of the magnitude of risks is derived by the governance structure from high-level qualitative judgments of likelihood and impact and is used to assess and prioritize risks at the enterprise level.	The organization has developed a prioritized portfolio of enterprise risks focused on business objectives and risks to, and opportunities for, those objectives both at the business unit level and at the enterprise level.	The organization maintains a prioritized portfolio of enterprise risks which are assessed in the context of the overall organization objectives. Risks at the program or process level allow decision-making based on a thorough understanding of top-down and bottom-up risks and interrelated risks.	The administration's prioritized portfolio is updated in real-time.

Source: Enterprise Risk Management Maturity Model OECD 2021.

ERM Performance – Risk Treatment Maturity:

EMERGING	PROGRESSING	ESTABLISHED	LEADING	ASPIRATIONAL
Risk treatment plans are not usually in place although high-level contingency plans may be drawn up for how the business unit or administration might to react to a few plausible risks if and when they materialize.	Risk treatment plans are developed at the business unit level in a standardized format which requires an assessment of the costs and benefits and an explanation of treatment choices. This will often be done in a subjective manner and will depend heavily on the engagement of senior management. As a result, there can be wide variations.	Risk treatments plans are developed in a standardized and data-informed manner at multiple levels of the organization with some degree of coordination across business units. These treatment plans take account of the business context; cost and benefits; obligations and expectations; prioritization of risks; risk appetite; risk severity; and residual risk.	The full range of potential risk treatment options, including for interrelated risks, are considered and tested in a cross-administration process. This includes the analysis and treatment of the risks resulting from a chosen risk treatment. Results are measured and triggers are identified and deployed to detect a need for adjustments to risk treatment approaches.	Risk treatment options are identified using an integrated risk assessment system using advanced technology tools to calculate cost and benefits against a wide set of risk parameters and data.
Monitoring is only performed through compliance and internal audit activities and most risk treatment information is only collected by individual areas of responsibility with only risk treatment on high-profile areas or projects reported to the governance bodies.	Risk treatments are put in place by each business unit and reported to the appropriate governance committees with periodic updating of the committees. There is limited validation outside of major projects or high.	There is regular centralized consideration and challenge of risk treatment proposals by the governance bodies with a focus on the enterprise level and higher risk projects. Risk treatment plans for enterprise risks are collected but may not be routinely shared across the administration.	The validation of risk treatment plans from across the units, including how they interrelate, is done in a joined-up process by the governance bodies and business units. The effectiveness of risk treatments is periodically tested. Consideration is given to when treatment may require the revision of a strategy or business objective.	Risk treatment options are continuously monitored in the light of new information, including their effectiveness, and recommendations for adjustments can be made in real time.

Source: Enterprise Risk Management Maturity Model OECD 2021.

ERM Review and Revision Maturity:

EMERGING	PROGRESSING	ESTABLISHED	LEADING	ASPIRATIONAL
Reviews are carried out in a reactive manner in the light of high-impact events occurring or where there has been serious reputational damage to the administration. Changes are generally confined to addressing the particular issue or business area rather than more systemic issues.	The effectiveness of ERM practices over the preceding year is assessed regularly in a general way as well as in the event of realized risks with significant adverse impacts.	Reviews are undertaken regularly of higher-risk business areas with detailed recommendations for any major improvements in particular business areas are made to the relevant responsible managers. Action plans are put in place as necessary and monitored by senior administration management.	ERM outcomes are reflected in regular business performance management processes, including in regular reporting to senior management. The effectiveness of administration wide ERM practices and capabilities is periodically assessed in a detailed manner and benchmarked against other organizations.	ERM outcomes are fully integrated into real-time business performance reporting. The effectiveness of ERM practices, capabilities, and treatments is assessed by advanced technology tools and subject to occasional independent review against leading practices.

Source: Enterprise Risk Management Maturity Model OECD 2021.

ERM Information, Communication, and Reporting Maturity:

EMERGING	PROGRESSING	ESTABLISHED	LEADING	ASPIRATIONAL
Risk information is extracted largely manually at the business unit level and the scope and relevance will depend on management engagement and expertise in particular business areas, leading to high variability across the organization and a largely reactive approach to ERM.	Risk management reporting templates and communication channels are defined, although not always consistently applied across the administration. While data is kept in electronic form, the variability in the quality and timeliness of information can impact the quality of decision-making, in particular, areas of interrelated risks.	The organization generally uses existing information and technology systems to capture what it needs to understand risk, make risk-aware decisions, and fulfil reporting requirements. Risk information standards and ownership are defined and various channels are available for communicating risk information to those with ERM responsibilities.	Categorized risk information, including a wide range of KPIs and KRIs, is integrated into enterprise architecture. High-quality, timely, and accurate data is integrated into the regular reporting and decision-making tools across the organization and can be pulled from a common data warehouse on demand by decision-makers and risk owners.	Advanced data analytics, such as artificial intelligence and data mining is leveraged to collect, convert, and analyze large volumes of data into clear and readily understandable risk management information to inform proactive decision-making. Such information is increasingly available in real-time and to staff across the organization.
In general, risk information outside of periodic high-level key performance indicators (KPIs) or key risk indicators (KRIs) are not communicated routinely to governance committees and is usually sent on request or where business unit management chooses to escalate issues, which will often be done inconsistently across the administration.	More detailed KPIs and KRIs are in place for all core business processes and are increasingly shared across business areas. Significant adverse changes in KPIs and KRIs will usually be triggers for further investigations and more detailed reporting to management and governance committees.	The format of reporting (including standard analytics, commentary, and the mapping of KPIs and KRIs to individual risks and objectives) enables business units to understand the relationships between risk and performance to improve decision-making. While reporting is consistent, data timeliness, accuracy, and quality vary across the business units.	Management routinely assesses, in close collaboration with report users, what information is required (both for decision-makers and staff more generally) how often reports are needed, and presentational preferences, with changes being made as necessary. There are dedicated methods to extract and report meaningful information on culture.	Increasingly the format of reporting can be tailored according to the requirements of particular users with functionality to undertake detailed drill-downs into risk parameters and interrelated risks. There is periodic evaluation of the effectiveness of the communication channels and functionality in ensuring that reporting is comprehensive, timely, and accurate.

Source: Enterprise Risk Management Maturity Model OECD 2021.

Appendix IV
Culture Assessment Survey

The following questions can be included in an Organizational Culture Assessment, asking the employee to rank how strongly they agree (or do not agree) with each statement using the typical scale:

- 1 Strongly Disagree
- 2 Disagree
- 3 Neutral
- 4 Agree
- 5 Strongly Agree

Mission and Values:

- The organization's mission is inclusive of many or all impacted stakeholders.
- I understand how my role/responsibilities impact the company's mission.
- I know and understand the organization's stated core values.
- I believe the organization's core values align with my individual values.
- I understand how the organization's strategic goals impact the mission.

- I understand how my functional/departmental goals support the organization's strategic goals.
- I believe leaders embody the organization's core values.

Performance Management and Compensation:

- Incentive programs are aligned with the organizational mission.
- Incentive programs are aligned with the organization's core values.
- Success (or failure) is clearly defined and communicated.
- Leaders award success consistently across the organization.
- Leaders address bad behavior consistently across the organization.
- Incentive programs encourage behaviors that are consistent with the organization's core values.
- The performance management process solicits input from managers, peers, and subordinates to achieve a more balanced feedback process.

Accountability:

- There are robust policies and procedures in place.
- Policies and procedures are clearly communicated to all employees.
- Employees understand how each policy or procedure impacts their role and responsibility.
- There are effective processes and systems in place to detect exceptions and outliers to expected performance or behaviors.
- Exceptions to expected performance or behaviors are addressed timely, appropriately, and consistently.
- There are consequences for not complying with company policies and procedures or to the organization's core values.
- Failure is viewed as an opportunity to continuously improve.

Communication and Transparency:

- There is a safe environment for open and transparent communication at all levels of the organization.
- Leaders encourage constructive criticism or challenges to the status quo in efforts to continuously improve.

- Information flows from top to bottom in an unrestricted and timely manner.
- Information flows from bottom to top in an unrestricted and timely manner.
- Information flows across the organization in an unrestricted and timely manner.
- Communication is generally accurate, complete, and consistent throughout the organization.
- Difficult conversations are used as opportunities to resolve conflict with positive intent.

Talent Management:

- Employees understand how their roles and responsibilities support the overall strategy.
- The talent acquisition process considers the organization's core values in the hiring of new employees.
- The organization has a process to evaluate employees' adherence to core values.
- The organization invests in training and development for employees.
- The organization's turnover is consistent with their industry peers.
- The organization has a process for assessing employee engagement on a regular basis.
- The organization is committed to addressing any gaps or areas of concern from the results of the employee engagement survey.

Risk Management:

- Enterprise risk management is aligned with and informs the organization's strategy.
- The organization has a defined risk appetite and related risk-tolerance thresholds.
- The enterprise risk management process is supported by the CEO and the executive team.
- The enterprise risk management progress and updates are reported to the board on a regular basis.

- Performance metrics (KPIs/KRIs) are used to measure and manage risks.
- Tolerable risk levels (what is acceptable vs unacceptable) are communicated to all employees as it relates to their role/responsibility.
- Employees understand how their decisions within their role/responsibility may impact the risk to the organization.

Leadership:

- My experience with the actual culture is consistent with how leaders describe the desired culture.
- Leaders are effective in addressing the gaps between the desired culture and the actual culture.
- Leaders consistently "walk the talk" as it relates to the organizational culture they espouse.
- Leaders ensure there is an environment that encourages open communication across, up, and down the organization.
- Leaders are hiring and promoting individuals that embody the organization's core values.
- Leaders hold all individuals accountable for their actions or lack of action.
- Leaders have an effective risk management process in place.

Appendix V
Culture Wellness Report Card

1		**Culture Assessment**					
	a.	Mission and Values	Strongly Disagree	Disagree	Neutral	Agree	Strongly Agree
	b.	Incentive Compensation	Strongly Disagree	Disagree	Neutral	Agree	Strongly Agree
	c.	Accountability	Strongly Disagree	Disagree	Neutral	Agree	Strongly Agree
	d.	Transparency	Strongly Disagree	Disagree	Neutral	Agree	Strongly Agree
	e.	Talent Management	Strongly Disagree	Disagree	Neutral	Agree	Strongly Agree
	f.	Risk Management	Strongly Disagree	Disagree	Neutral	Agree	Strongly Agree
	g.	Leadership	Strongly Disagree	Disagree	Neutral	Agree	Strongly Agree
2		**Policy Management Maturity**	Ad Hoc	Fragmented	Defined	Integrated	Agile
3		**Process Maturity**	Ad Hoc	Repeatable	Defined	Managed	Optimized
4		**Talent Management**:					
	a.	Employee Engagement Survey (for example)	Strongly Disagree	Disagree	Neutral	Agree	Strongly Agree
5		**Industry Benchmarking Metrics**:					
	a.	Turnover rate *(for example)*	Significant Negative Variance	Negative Variance	Consistent with peers	Positive Variance	Significant Positive Variance
6		**External Feedback**:					
	a.	Glassdoor Rating *(for example)*	1	2	3	4	5
7		**ERM Process Maturity**	Emerging	Progressing	Established	Leading	Aspirational

Appendix VI
Culture Assessment Attributes

- Organizational Culture Assessment
- Policy Management Maturity
- Process Maturity
- Talent management metrics:
    - Employee Engagement Survey
    - Employee Relation Complaints
    - Performance Appraisal Scores
    - Turnover Rate
    - Exit Interviews
    - Training
    - Ethics Hotline
- Industry Peers
- Other External Feedback:
    - Customers
    - Former Employees
    - External Auditors
    - Consultants
    - Vendors
    - Recruiters
    - General Public
- Enterprise Risk Management Process Maturity

Appendix VII
Common Categories of Root Causes

The following categories are the root causes for employees to not comply with organizational policies, procedures, or expected standards:

- Lack of effective policies: employees did not know what the company rules are.
- Lack of effective procedures: employees did not know how the rules impact their day-to-day operations in their individual roles and responsibilities.
- Lack of effective communication: employees did not receive information about them in a timely or effective manner.
- Lack of effective training: employees did not understand how to practically implement the policies and procedures.
- Lack of prioritization: employees did not prioritize compliance to a rule (e.g., due to competing priorities).
- Lack of management monitoring: managers did not prioritize their attention and focus on employees' compliance to rules (e.g., managers were incentivized to prioritize a competing objective).
- Lack of resources: leaders did not prioritize the resources (e.g., budget, people, tools, etc.) needed to comply with the rules.

Depending on which root cause is the reason for a failure to comply with expected performance, it may be a simple fix such as documenting or formalizing policies and procedures; or it could be much more complex to resolve in terms of prioritizing competing objectives and aligning everyone, from top to bottom, towards the same strategic goals. Processes are easy to change. People's behaviors and motivations are much more difficult to influence.

Index

Pages in **bold** refer to tables.

For Product Safety Concerns and Information please contact our EU
representative GPSR@taylorandfrancis.com
Taylor & Francis Verlag GmbH, Kaufingerstraße 24, 80331 München, Germany

www.ingramcontent.com/pod-product-compliance
Ingram Content Group UK Ltd.
Pitfield, Milton Keynes, MK11 3LW, UK
UKHW020207200926
475702UK00004B/655

* 9 7 8 1 0 3 2 2 6 5 4 6 9 *